# Miss Confederation

JUN 1 5 2017

971.049092 Coles -M

McDonald, A.
Miss Confederation.

PRICE: $22.99 (3559/he )

# Miss Confederation

## The Diary of Mercy Anne Coles

ANNE McDONALD

Foreword by Christopher Moore

DUNDURN
TORONTO

Copyright © Anne McDonald, 2017

All rights reserved. No part of this publication may be reproduced, stored in a retrieval system, or transmitted in any form or by any means, electronic, mechanical, photocopying, recording, or otherwise (except for brief passages for purpose of review) without the prior permission of Dundurn Press. Permission to photocopy should be requested from Access Copyright.

Cover images: main image — I-13486.1 | Photograph | Miss Mercy Coles, Montreal, QC, 1864 | © McCord Museum; background painting — Dusan Kadlec, *Province House Ball 1864*
Printer: Webcom

**Library and Archives Canada Cataloguing in Publication**

McDonald, Anne, 1960-, author
Miss Confederation : the diary of Mercy Anne Coles / Anne McDonald.

Includes bibliographical references and index.
Issued in print and electronic formats.
ISBN 978-1-4597-3967-3 (softcover).--ISBN 978-1-4597-3968-0 (PDF).--
ISBN 978-1-4597-3969-7 (EPUB)

1. Coles, Mercy Anne, 1838-1921. 2. Coles, Mercy Anne, 1838-1921--Diaries. 3. Women--Canada--History--19th century. 4. Women--Canada--Diaries. 5. Women--Canada--Biography. 6. Canada--Biography. 7. Prince Edward Island--Biography. 8. Canada--History--Confederation, 1867. I. Title.

FC471.C645M3 2017 971.04'9092 C2017-901267-3
C2017-901268-1

1 2 3 4 5 21 20 19 18 17

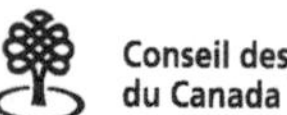

Canada Council for the Arts

We acknowledge the support of the **Canada Council for the Arts** and the **Ontario Arts Council** for our publishing program. We also acknowledge the financial support of the **Government of Ontario**, through the **Ontario Book Publishing Tax Credit** and the **Ontario Media Development Corporation**, and the **Government of Canada**.

Care has been taken to trace the ownership of copyright material used in this book. The author and the publisher welcome any information enabling them to rectify any references or credits in subsequent editions.
*— J. Kirk Howard, President*

The publisher is not responsible for websites or their content unless they are owned by the publisher.

Printed and bound in Canada.

VISIT US AT

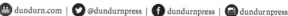

 dundurn.com | 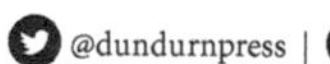 @dundurnpress | dundurnpress | dundurnpress

Dundurn
3 Church Street, Suite 500
Toronto, Ontario, Canada
M5E 1M2

*For my mother, Audrey McDonald,*
*from whom I've inherited my curiosity*
*and interest in the "real" story,*
*and my aunt, Frances McDonald Griffith (1922–2011),*
*who shared with me her essays and research on*
*the history of Prince Edward Island, from*
*out-migration to Francis Bolger's seminal work.*

# Contents

# Foreword

## by Christopher Moore

For years I had a little crush on Miss Mercy Coles, even when I only knew her diary from nasty print-outs and photocopies from the archives. When a well-brought-up Island girl would let me read her private thoughts, how could I not be smitten? The lively little scenes she conjures up, the bitter disappointments she confesses, the sharp opinions she offers — they all captivated me.

How could my heart not melt when illness strikes her down just before the elegant ball she has set her heart on? A triumphal appearance might have changed her life. Alas, she missed it.

How could I resist her vivid pen sketches of the great men of confederation? John A. Macdonald brings her dessert. Charles Tupper bustles in with his medical bag. D'Arcy McGee takes her to dinner and then drinks too much. Her own politician father dances himself into a lather. All this is livelier than, say, the debate over Number 8 of the Quebec Conference's seventy-two constitutional resolutions. Such matters Mercy declines to mention, though her father is in the thick of them, and one senses she knows a good deal about them.

But … I was being selfish, too. Mostly, I plundered what Mercy would tell me. I was greedy for the glimpses she gave of history in the making. Really, I was not paying attention to her hopes and dreams at all. I was just there to grab what I could use.

Men!

Anne McDonald taught me the error of my ways. It was from her sensitive reading in this book that I came truly to appreciate Mercy Anne Coles, Miss Confederation. It is Anne McDonald who listens for what a young woman of the 1860s will not say in words. She teaches us how to see all that is hiding between Mercy's lines.

Any reader can note that Leonard Tilley, the premier of New Brunswick, is a fellow passenger on the Coles family's slow train to Quebec City. Anne McDonald sees and shows us the courting rituals that may be linking Mercy to this dynamic, and youngish, widower. And when the Coles family dines with John A. Macdonald, also a widower, she is the one who asks whether Mercy considers him as husband material. Those ambitious young political aides constantly about the hotel parlour — do they stand a chance at all?

Anne McDonald lets us see that the gender politics around the Quebec Conference are at least as subtle as the constitutional partnership that is being negotiated simultaneously.

Mercy Anne Coles's diary is far and away the most personal account we have of the events surrounding the making of Canada's confederation in 1864. Anne McDonald, herself an Island girl, almost, is our ideal guide to it. She unobtrusively gives us all the background we might want. More than that, she *listens* to Mercy. She suggests what we might look for, just below the surface of the text.

*Christopher Moore has twice won the Governor General's Literary Award. He is the author of* 1867: How the Fathers Made a Deal *and* Three Weeks in Quebec City: The Meeting That Made Canada, *among many other works. Mercy Coles plays cameo roles in both.*

# Preface

Prince Edward Island is always thought of as the birthplace of Confederation because the politicians of the day, including Canada's first prime minister, John A. Macdonald, met in Charlottetown to discuss the possibility of a political union of the colonies of British North America. Thoughts of union had been bandied about for years, but it was in Charlottetown that it looked like the idea would finally take hold.

That was in the late summer of 1864, and the weather, which would normally have turned cool by September first, was unseasonably warm. Not only was Prince Edward Island playing host to the politicians who had come to talk union, but, amazingly enough, the first circus in almost a generation had just arrived in Charlottetown. The Islanders, it turned out, including the PEI politicians, were more interested in the circus than in the negotiations to unite the colonies. You can't blame them. The late summer was as lovely as summer can be in what's come to be known as Canada's Garden Province, and the circus was the highlight of the season.

I learned all this one unreasonably hot summer in Toronto when I was teaching an adult English as Another Language literacy class, with students from all over the world. On a whim one sleepy afternoon, all of us sweltering together in an old school without air conditioning, the class watched a video celebrating Canada's 125th birthday. The video told the story of the PEI Father of Confederation William Pope being rowed out in a tiny boat to the steamship *Queen Victoria* to meet the men who had come from Canada to PEI to talk Confederation.

I was astonished. My father was from Prince Edward Island. As children, my sisters and I had gone almost every summer to visit my grandmother and aunts and uncles there. I love the Island, and I love history, and I'd never heard any of this before.

I knew I had found a story I wanted to write.

I began an enormous amount of research, and, in the course of doing so, I heard an interview on CBC Radio with Christopher Moore. He mentioned a young woman from PEI named Mercy Anne Coles. She had gone with her father, George Coles, to the Confederation conference in Quebec City in October 1864, which followed the summer meeting in Charlottetown. Mercy was one of nine unmarried daughters (only daughters went, no sons) of Maritime delegates who went to Quebec, where the now-famous Fathers of Confederation met to work out the terms for this union of all the British colonies.

And she'd kept a diary of her trip.

It was the Canadians, those from present-day Quebec and Ontario, who were most in need of a political union. At that conference in Quebec City they wanted to do everything in their power to charm the Maritime delegates. They must have realized it was crucial to keep the relaxed, convivial tone and lovely party atmosphere of Charlottetown going. And for that to happen, they knew they needed to include the women. Not only were the belles of Quebec City invited to the banquets and balls that were held alongside the political discussions, so too were the wives, sisters, and daughters of the Maritime delegates. In this way, the Canadians could court the Maritimers, and the Maritimers would be able to enjoy a sightseeing- and banquet-filled trip of a lifetime, at which their daughters could "come out."

There are newspaper accounts of the events, banquets, and balls in Quebec City; speeches published months after the meetings; letters from George Brown (founder of the *Globe*, today's *Globe and Mail*) to his wife; and limited minutes of the proceedings — all written by men. The story of the women who were present at the Confederation conference events has been absent from the record. Mercy Coles's diary gives us that story.

I have transcribed the full diary, all of which is included in this book. Mercy's two weeks of travel back home to PEI through the northern United States while the Civil War was in full swing, which has never been documented before now, is also included. This latter part of the diary was a revealing read; it captures a different side of Mercy, perhaps a more vulnerable side.

We are so lucky to have Mercy Coles's diary. She thought to keep a record of the events, and just as importantly, she thought to preserve that record and pass it on to relatives. They, in turn, were wise enough to take care of it, and eventually share it with Library and Archives Canada.

It is the only full account of these events from a woman's perspective. Further, it's not tied to political ideals or machinations. It is a record caught at the moment history was being made, without the veneer or gloss that passing time creates.

---

When I first read the diary, I focused on the parts that were easy to read and transcribe, and used the events and timeline loosely in my novel *To the Edge of the Sea*, set during the Confederation conferences. It was a few years afterward that I began transcribing the full diary, reading it closely, paying attention to every nuance, and looking at the placement of words on the page.

Mercy was often travelling while she wrote — bumping along on the trains or in a carriage, and so, especially in the latter part of her diary, there are words and phrases that are illegible at points.

Because it is an original document, one can see Mercy's style of writing and penmanship; they became an interest in and of themselves. I had to work closely with the text to understand what she was saying. For example, I wondered to whom she was referring when she wrote "Lala dined with us.... I was rather disappointed in the man...." Whomever she was speaking of was obviously famous, but who was he? Not the yellow Teletubby, I was sure. A study of Mercy's penmanship proved it was "Sala" I needed to look for, not "Lala." Ah — it was George Augustus Sala, a British journalist, famous at the time, who was then travelling through Canada.

One can see how Mercy shapes her capital *S*, and *R*. The *S* is important to identifying Sala's name. Her capital *R* is distinctive, closer to what is typically a small *r*, but made large enough to be a capital letter. The name Louis Riel comes out clearly, even though it is small in size, written to fit in the same line as "a Red River man," but above it. It's clear that the name was written some time *afterward*. How long afterward, though? It could very well have been later that same day. Still, the fact that it is an *unknown* time afterwards is important for assessing the accuracy of what Mercy knew at the time, and what she believed later. Even within this original document, then, it can be seen how the passing of time and the impulse of the author to edit her work have affected the history of the moment.

---

More than the study of the writing, though, it was the people, places, and events Mercy wrote of that interested me. At every turn, she piqued my curiosity. What were her relationships with John A. Macdonald or with Leonard Tilley? Why was the Victoria Bridge an important part of their sightseeing itinerary — and was that the same bridge we'd crossed over every week when I was a child to go visit my cousins in Montreal? Was diphtheria, which Mercy caught in Quebec City, really that bad? What was this "Bonnie Blue Flag" she wrote of while visiting with her relatives in Ohio?

I was intrigued by all she wrote. As I researched further, I felt like I was recreating a picture of Canada as it was at Confederation, a picture framed and circumscribed by what Mercy Coles presented to me, as it was presented to her. It is by no means a complete picture — it is, as I say, a circumscribed view of the time, the events, places, and people at an important time in Canada's history. Importantly, Mercy has given immediacy, colour, and depth to all to which she turned her gaze, her female gaze.

That this is the first time the diary will have been published is extraordinary to me. Pieces of it have been quoted, but it has never been published in its entirety. That it hasn't appeared until now speaks volumes about who and what we consider worthy of hearing. It is heartening that now, 150 years later, Mercy Coles's writing will be available to all.

Reminiscences
of
Canada
in
1864.
by
Mercy Coles.

Wednesday 5th Oct/64
Left Ch Town at 3 A. M. arrived at Shediac at ½ past 2. I was very ill. it was so rough. Monk came off in a small boat & was taken on board of Summerside found a special Train waiting for us at Shediac, arrived at St John at ½ past 6. Mr Tilly & Mr Steves at the Hotel to receive us. Ma. Pa. Mr Tilly & I went to see Mrs Perley. Mr Tilly did not come
Thursday — We had a walk before breakfast came on board New Brunswick, I am going to share a stateroom with Mrs Alexander arrived at Eastport at 12. went on shore & dined. left at 1 - for Portland
Friday morning. Portland, "Preble House." we arrived here this morning after being 24 hours.

on board the New Brunswick. I went to bed at 6 & was just up in time this moring. we had an awful stormy night. we leave here in the Grand Trunk Railway at 1 oclock, we parted with Mr Harnes at the wharf he was very attentive & kind.

Saturday 5th. We arrived at Island Pond last night at ¼ past 9. we got up this moring at ½ past 4. we have just started in Cars again & one might just as well try to write on horseback. we saw some beautiful scenery yesterday coming through New Hampshire it was too dark to see the White Mountains. Mr Tilly helped me admire it. It is rather a joke he is the only beau of the party

*One*

# Miss Confederation: Mercy Anne Coles

*It is rather a joke, he is the only beau of the party and with 5 single ladies he has something to do to keep them all in good humour.*[1]

THE "HE" MENTIONED IN THE ABOVE QUOTATION IS LEONARD TILLEY, who was then the premier of New Brunswick, and Mercy Anne Coles, the irreverent writer of this note, was one of those single women. Ten unmarried women altogether, three from Prince Edward Island, two from Nova Scotia, four from New Brunswick, and one from Canada West, accompanied their fathers or brothers to the conference in Quebec City, where the men negotiated Confederation and the creation of Canada.

The start of Canada's journey to Confederation is a fascinating one, involving a circus; Farini, the tightrope walker from Port Hope, Ontario; the American Civil War; a whole lot of champagne, sunshine, and sea; and lovemaking — in the old-fashioned sense.

The process began in earnest when, in September 1864, the Fathers of Confederation, travelling by rail, steamship, and horse-drawn carriage, met in Charlottetown, the provincial capital of Prince Edward Island, to discuss the possibility of a union of Britain's North American colonies.* Like New Brunswick, Nova Scotia, and Newfoundland, PEI was an independent colony of the British Crown at the time. The final of this group of colonies, Canada, was made up of Ontario and Quebec, then known respectively as Canada West and Canada East. Each of the Maritime colonies was very small, and with a large and growing American neighbour, many of the colonies' residents, including those of Canada East and West, felt that if they were to survive separate from the United States, then the time had come to join forces and form a larger political entity.**

Following their time in Charlottetown, the Canadian and Maritime delegates crossed the Northumberland Strait on the Canadians' steamship, the *Queen Victoria*, and toured briefly through Nova Scotia and New Brunswick, meeting in Halifax on September 12 for the delegates to discuss the idea of Confederation further. Mercy Coles, the unmarried twenty-six-year-old daughter of Prince Edward Island delegate George Coles, went with her father on this tour. From Mercy's descriptions she was the only young woman to go on this trip with the delegates. Perhaps her father viewed this as an opportunity for her education, or to meet a potential husband.

The big meetings and events, though, were saved for Quebec City, where, in October 1864, the Maritime Fathers of Confederation, with their unmarried daughters and sisters in tow, travelled again on the *Queen Victoria*, which the Canadians had sent to bring the Maritimers up to Quebec City. They promenaded on the decks and looked out at the spectacular fall scenery along the shores of the St. Lawrence.

---

* No young women from New Brunswick, Nova Scotia, or Canada, accompanied their fathers to the Charlottetown conference in September 1864. No doubt the men didn't view the time in Prince Edward Island (which had nowhere near the opportunities and entertainment that Quebec City had) as an opportunity for their daughters to meet potential husbands. The women of PEI, however, including Mercy Coles and Margaret Gray, were part of the social events at Charlottetown.

** Newfoundland did not take part in the Charlottetown conference, however representatives from there did go to the Quebec conference.

Mercy Coles was not part of this large group, however. She writes that her "father thought the trip [by ship the whole way] would be too rough for mother and me."[2] Instead, Mercy, her father and mother; William Pope (Colonial Secretary and a member of the Conservative Party, which was in power in PEI) and his wife; and Mrs. Alexander, the widowed sister of Thomas Heath Haviland (also a member of the Conservative Party), left on October 5, a day earlier than the others. They crossed from PEI to Shediac, New Brunswick, then took a train specially booked for them to Saint John. There they picked up Leonard Tilley, the aforementioned "only beau of the party," as well as two members of Tilley's government — Charles Fisher, with his daughter Jane, and William Steeves, with his two daughters.

From Saint John, they travelled by steamship down the Bay of Fundy, the trip taking twenty-four hours, to Portland, Maine (compare this to the sixty-plus hours it would take to get to Quebec City by ship). There was as yet no rail line from the Maritimes to Quebec through Canada, and so the group had to take this roundabout route through the United States. Of course, what the single women missed in the promenading on the *Queen Victoria's* deck, they gained in the attention paid to them by the recent widower and then-premier of New Brunswick, Leonard Tilley.

In Quebec City, the Fathers debated and finally crafted the seventy-two resolutions of the British North America Act, the act that formed the Canadian constitution at the time, and which still forms the basis of the Canadian constitution today.

---

Politics was not the only thing on the minds of those discussing the creation of Confederation, however. The men viewed the conference and following tour of the Canadas as a wonderful opportunity for other matters; they brought along their unmarried daughters and sisters to … well, to promote unions of a different sort. Luckily for us, Mercy Coles kept a diary of her trip. She wrote of her travels and of the events, balls, banquets, people, and whirlwind of social happenings and political manoeuvrings as they affected her and her desires.

The diary has never been published, and yet without it, Confederation history is — no question — incomplete. It is not the only such document, however: George Brown was one of the Canadian delegates, and the discovery, in the 1950s, of his letters to his wife, Anne, written during the Confederation conferences provided greater understanding of what made the union possible. The letters document the important relationships that were forged, and how those connections affected the views and attitudes of the delegates. The Mercy Coles diary also offers important insight into the people present at the Quebec conference, and provides the only report by a Canadian female of Canada's social and political landscape in 1864.

———

Mercy Anne Coles was the third child of George Coles and his wife, Mercy Haine Coles. The couple had twelve children, two of whom, a boy and a girl, died in infancy. Their first nine children were girls. George Coles was a prosperous merchant, brewer, and distiller. In 1851, he led the Reform party to victory, and was PEI's first premier. He led the government from 1851 to1854, and then, after six months out of office, from 1854 to 1859. Best known as the man who achieved responsible government for PEI in 1851, Coles was the leader of the Reform or Liberal Party, which was mostly supported by Roman Catholics, though Coles himself was Anglican. That he was able to muster such support, even in the face of the divisive issues that often fell along the religious lines of his time, is a tribute to the esteem in which Prince Edward Islanders held him, and is indicative of their support for his policies.

Coles was a self-made man, not one of the wealthy landowners whose politics tended to support absentee landlords and kept the many tenant farmers of PEI in a state of poverty. His government launched many remarkably progressive measures, such as the Free Education Act, which was passed in 1852. This act — the first in British North America, and possibly the first of this type of act in all of Britain's colonies — provided free education for all primary school–aged children. The government also created a provincial fund to pay teachers' salaries.

In contrast, other conference attendees from PEI, such as Colonel John Hamilton Gray, who was the premier of PEI in 1864, and Thomas

Heath Haviland, who was among the ruling landowners, would have had different expectations and different values from those of Coles, just as their daughters and sisters would have also had different expectations and values from those held by Mercy.

---

These sharp differences in outlook and expectations existed despite the fact that all hailed from the relatively small city of Charlottetown. In 1838, the year Mercy was born, Charlottetown was a city with a population of just over three thousand people; although its population had doubled since then, it was still just over 6,700 in 1861. The province itself had a population of 80,552 by 1861, having grown in size by over thirty thousand people in the previous twenty-six years.

Like other cities at the time, Charlottetown had dirt streets that in the fall and spring were mired in mud. The *Islander* reported on April 14, 1863, that women, "on their way to church, [were] floundering about in the mud like swine in a hog-sty."[3] They'd get so stuck they had to have men pull them out. Even in much larger places, like Quebec City, which had a population of fifty thousand, the situation was similar. "You cannot put a foot off the sidewalk without plunging into mud," wrote the correspondent for the Montreal newspaper *La Minerve* about Quebec City on Sunday, October 10, 1864,[4] the day the delegates arrived on the *Queen Victoria.*

Prince Edward Island was almost entirely rural in the 1860s, and agriculture was, by far, the most important part of the economy. Only about 9 percent of the population lived in the capital city. There were reportedly 800 cattle, 850 sheep, 350 horses, and 400 hogs living in Charlottetown in 1861. Animals roamed the streets, and boys were hired to keep stray animals off them.[5]

Things were bad enough on normal days, but on days when the market was held, the situation became significantly worse. The market house, which at the time was in a serious state of dilapidation, was located in Queen Square — the same place that the seat of government, Province House, was located. Their proximity to each other caused a great deal of chagrin in many of the local politicians. Held twice weekly, year-round, the market was renowned for its filth: animal excrement, fish guts, and more littered the ground. Most of the vendors chose to sell their wares and produce outside, rather than be stuck inside the building. Even more filth and noise was the result.

It is of little surprise, then, that epidemics of cholera, typhus, smallpox, and typhoid were far from uncommon in Charlottetown. And although these types of epidemics were commonplace in other cities in British North America at this time, their impact was especially severe in Charlottetown, as there was no permanent hospital there until 1879.

In winter, the mail came and left by iceboat. Such trips were, at times, dangerous, and it was often questionable whether the mail would arrive at all. Evelyn MacLeod, in her annotations of the 1863 diary of Margaret Gray (the eighteen-year-old daughter of PEI's premier, Colonel John Hamilton Gray), describes the small boats: "[They were] approximately seventeen feet long and four feet wide, and covered with heavy tin. Leather straps harnessed men to the boat as they hauled it across solid ice, and oars and sometimes a sail were used in patches of open water." In describing the difficulties of receiving or sending mail, MacLeod quotes the Charlottetown *Guardian* on March 13, 1863: "Several attempts have been made during the week to cross the Straits but owing to the bad state of the ice they have proved ineffectual."[6]

The ice often didn't melt until the middle or end of April, and so shortages of many goods were common by the end of winter. As Margaret Gray wrote, the shops were close to empty by March.[7] With no (or very slow) mail in or out, and no goods till the ice broke up and allowed steamers back into the harbour, Islanders were forced to be very self-sufficient.

---

The consequent privation that many in the province experienced was less of an issue for the Coles family, however, because of its large size and relative affluence. Also, although George Coles owned a brewery and distillery in town, the Coleses' home was Stone Park Farm, on the outskirts of the city. It was four kilometres from Province House, and Mercy and her sisters were spared some of the day-to-day difficulties of living in town.

Despite the fact that they lived outside of the city, Coles's daughters still benefitted from the education and culture that would have been more easily available to their urban peers. It's likely that tutors came to the house, and the young women may have gone out to get specialized lessons in such things as singing. Margaret Gray, likewise, wrote that a tutor came to teach her and her sisters German, and that they went out for singing lessons. As well as such formal instruction, Coles's daughters would also have been exposed to the sort of informal tuition offered by the lively discussions held in their home. George Coles would have entertained his political allies, and perhaps the discussions included the women of the household, as the Coles sisters were noted to be "well educated, well informed and sharp as needles."[8]

---

Such is the background of Mercy Coles. It is important to keep this in mind, because this Confederation story is one told from a young, unmarried woman's point of view. It is a story told by someone along for the events, and tied in that way to the goings-on. Yet, Mercy Coles was interested in something far different from the resolutions of the British North America Act. She was twenty-six, after all, when twenty-six was getting old to be single.* Mercy had seven surviving sisters altogether. Her two older sisters were already married, and of the two just younger than she, Eliza was about to be married in December, and the other one already was. The next in line after that was already twenty years old. Thus, the pressure was on, and Mercy's interest in the men she met during this time is not surprising. Many of the men, including John A. Macdonald, were taken with her. And here she was with a bevy of single women, younger and thus perhaps more desirable than herself, vying for the attention of Canada's foremost bachelors.

In her Confederation photograph, taken by the celebrated Montreal photographer William Notman, Mercy's eyes gaze back at the viewer with

* It wouldn't be uncommon then for women to marry in their late twenties, but given Mercy's situation with her many sisters and no apparent suitor in sight for her, we can see that she was feeling the pressure of time and opportunity.

intensity and interest. Her long, dark hair, thick with curl, is parted in the middle and pulled back from her brow, in the style of the day. She liked to have fun, to dance, to sing. She was easy to talk to. She liked teasing and being teased. Her wide mouth and full lips must have smiled easily. Men found her intelligent and attractive, especially in her "irresistible blue silk."[9] They paid attention to her. And she definitely enjoyed receiving their attention — but then, who doesn't, when they're young and looking for love?

And that's what she was doing — amid the grand and heady spectacle of the balls, banquets, and events that went along with the Confederation Conference of October 1864, in Quebec City. It was the perfect place for such a quest, because that city was the headiest of places in Canada then, with its corps of officers, garrison of British soldiers in red uniforms, and regimental bands. It was the hub of cultural and diplomatic life, and the most debonair of any of Canada's cities. Quebec City was, and is, strikingly beautiful, sitting atop a cliff, overlooking the St. Charles and St. Lawrence Rivers. The streets of the old city are cobblestoned, and wind crookedly past buildings and houses that look more European than North American.

Even amid the wonders of Quebec City and the conference events, however, it's clear that the country's politics affected Mercy Coles, too. This tale of the "Road to Confederation" is one shaped by a young female traveller interested in what all young people are interested in: falling in love, finding a mate, the excitement of travel, and the lure of "away." It is the *her*story of Confederation.

Mercy is refreshingly honest, and writes so blithely of people and events that we are caught in the moment in time at which history was being made, without the veneer and gloss time can create. We are allowed an intimate view into the past at this seminal period in Canada's history, and at the men, now famous, or once famous and now forgotten, who shaped Canada's future. Further, we're exposed to a female voice at the making of Confederation.

Women were not part of any official delegation, but the importance of connections to, and relationships with, women was recognized by those who were, and so it was that women had an unofficial role in the negotiations. As PEI delegate Edward Whelan noted for his newspaper, the *Examiner*:

Mercy Coles, October 29, 1864.

> The Cabinet Ministers — the leading ones especially — are the most inveterate dancers I have ever seen, they do not seem to miss a dance the live-long night. They are cunning fellows; and there is no doubt it is all done for a political purpose; they know if they can dance themselves into the affections of the wives and daughters of the country, the men will certainly become an easy conquest.[10]

Mercy's writings of the attention she received from men like John A. Macdonald and Leonard Tilley help us understand how the relationships at play worked to make Confederation a possibility.

In her diary, Mercy is willing to gossip; she's open; she's flirtatious. And yet she also shows a conventional side, happy to follow the strictures and guidelines expected of a young, single woman — but, interestingly, this is found mostly later in her diary, once the conference tour, and the possibility of her being wooed by any of the bachelors, has ended. Throughout, she maintains a sense of propriety — for example, she never mentions the first names of the other young women who attended the Confederation conference. Even when Emma Tupper and Margaret Gray visit her sickroom, she refers to them as "Miss Tupper" and "Miss Gray."

As Mary McDonald-Rissanen points out in her recent work on Prince Edward Island women diarists, *In the Interval of the Wave*, young women at that time would have read a lot of "comportment" literature, books written to teach young women how to behave properly. Yet, Mercy Coles also gossips and is flirtatious in her behaviour, and we only know that because she's written about it herself. Keeping a diary or journal is often used as a way to envision oneself, a way to create a self-identity through discovering oneself by writing. In the lively, breezy way in which she wrote, Mercy was definitely creating an image of herself, of how she wanted to be seen and how she wanted life to be.

In the 1860s, keeping a journal or diary was a way to achieve a level of independence, or at least the freedom to express one's thoughts, even if only in writing. Diary-keeping was recognized as a genre fit for women, but only if there were no intention of publishing the writing. Thus, women were free from scrutiny in their private journals, and could even subvert society's roles and ideals in playing at the creation of themselves.* Mercy Coles was free to invent this persona who did not, in her writing life, behave as conventionally as she sometimes behaved in real life.

Taking the time to keep a journal or diary showed an awareness of the self, of one's own story as unique from those of others, one that was worthy and important enough to record, even if it was only meant for oneself. It was also an indication of status: the woman who did this had enough time of her own, not absorbed by domestic duties, to write.

As the decades passed after Confederation, Mercy Coles obviously felt her diary was worthy of more attention than hers alone. Not only did she preserve it carefully, she took the time to share her stories and knowledge of Canada's beginnings with others, such as in a Charlottetown *Guardian* newspaper article published in 1917 about her time in Quebec City.

The diary is everything one wants it to be: it's gossipy, detailed, and full of social commentary. It is part travelogue, filled with detailed descriptions of her family's travels across Canada, and then through the U.S. states of Ohio, Pennsylvania, and New York on their return trip home to PEI. It covers the period from October 5, 1864, when she and her parents leave Charlottetown, to Thursday, November 17, 1864, when they return. Mercy writes of her sea-sick travel across the Northumberland Strait, and her journey by rail and ship to Quebec, all the single women flirting with Leonard Tilley, or vice versa.

The diary also covers the days of the conference itself, which began on October 10 and continued until October 26, with plenty of balls, banquets, parties, and outings — to court both the women and the Maritime delegates. The times, both politically and literally, were not quite as "sunny" as they'd been in Charlottetown, particularly for Prince Edward Island, which ended up opting out of the initial Confederation of New Brunswick, Nova Scotia, Quebec, and Ontario. And the weather was appalling.

* There has been a lot of academic research on the subject of women and the creation of identity through life writing. *The Small Details of Life: 20 Diaries by Women in Canada, 1830–1996*, edited by Kathryn Carter, Helen M. Buss's *Mapping Our Selves: Canadian Women's Autobiography in English*, and Felicity A. Nussbaum's article "Towards Conceptualizing Diary" in *Studies in Autobiography* are useful in understanding the area.

After the conference and tour of the Canadas ended, the Coles family continued on, through the United States, to visit with Mercy's mother's relatives. There, they travelled by train through cities busy drilling for oil and visited relatives caught up in the Civil War and the presidential election (Lincoln was re-elected just five months before he was assassinated), finally arriving at New York City — as bustling and busy then as it is now. Following their stay in New York, they travelled to Boston, and then returned to Prince Edward Island by steamer, meeting a couple forced to flee Atlanta, where their home had just been shelled by General Sherman in his "March to the Sea."

The Mercy Coles diary gives us a direct look back in time. Her breezy notations, with their lack of pretence, give every indication that she didn't intend her diary to be published, and that she wasn't thinking about how what she wrote might sound later, after people had died, or events had become significant. With its simple, unaffected tone, the diary seems to offer the reader the possibility of a clear view of the past.

This seeming straightforwardness is not quite as simple as it seems, however. Things are complicated by the fact that another version of the diary exists. The Charlottetown *Guardian* published a piece entitled "Reminiscences of Confederation Days: Extracts from a Diary Kept by Miss Mercy A. Coles When She Accompanied Her Father, the Late Hon. George Coles, to the Confederation Conferences at Quebec, Montreal and Ottawa in 1864," on June 30, 1917.* It was the fiftieth anniversary of Confederation in 1917, and the First World War was raging. Many thousands of Canadians had been killed, and the now seventy-nine-year-old Mercy Coles may have hoped to lighten the spirits of her fellow Islanders and offer some distraction from the war by recalling long-ago events. She may also have thought it was an opportunity to share her knowledge of the history of Prince Edward Island and her family. She had preserved her diary those many long years, and she didn't want it to be forgotten.

---

* The full newspaper article is reprinted in the Appendix. As well, much of the additional information has been added and noted as such in the transcription of the full original diary presented here.

In this newspaper extract of 1917, Mercy definitely takes more care with what she says than she had in her original accounts. There are significant differences between the newspaper article and the handwritten diary. First, the newspaper account is only an excerpt. Further, there are notable omissions from this newspaper extract, such as how miserable Mercy found Quebec City, and about D'Arcy McGee getting drunk at a dinner. These omissions may have resulted from Mercy censoring herself, or they may have been the product of actions by the editors of the *Guardian*. Another difference, even though much of the diary is quoted word for word, is the many places in which the events are told in past tense in a type of summary. Again, whether this was done by Mercy Coles herself or the newspaper isn't known. The result of this summarizing is that the diary loses some of its immediacy and vividness. There are also errors, such as in the name of the hotel in Quebec City at which the Coles family stayed.

Interestingly, there are also additions to the newspaper extract not contained in the handwritten diary, such as the reason why Mercy and her family did not travel to Quebec City on the *Queen Victoria*, the muddiness of D'Arcy McGee's riding in Montreal, and the wonderful hotel room John A. Macdonald arranged for her in Montreal. Perhaps these are remembrances or afterthoughts; still, the existence of these additional notes is curious, and one wonders if another version of the diary might exist, and what other extra notes there might be. The newspaper extract is also the only place where Mercy documents the brief tour through New Brunswick and Nova Scotia from September 8 to 18 that the delegates and she took after the Charlottetown conference ended on September 8, 1864.

Mercy's momentous trip was six weeks in length, and the diary entries, ten thousand words long, were written in a small, blue, hardcover book. The entries are often brief, with fleeting references to events, people, and places — they are, to some extent, similar to our social media postings of today. If, however, we pay close attention to Mercy's writings, and explore them in a deeper way than we would such postings, we can (re)learn what was considered of significance in 1864.

So, pour yourselves a bumper or two (or more) of champagne, have your booster shot for diphtheria, and come along on this Confederation ride.

*Two*

# Charlottetown: The Circus, Champagne, and Union

Thursday September 1, 1864, was a momentous day in Canadian history, the start to one long, sun-drenched, champagne- and circus-filled party.

On September 1, the Fathers of Confederation landed in Charlottetown, Prince Edward Island, to almost complete indifference, to talk about the possibility of a union of the British Provinces, or Confederation.

There was certainly political indifference, as it was the Canadians themselves who had wrangled an invite to a Maritime conference discussing a Maritime Union. The Maritimers weren't interested in that union either, but were forced to consider the proposal by Arthur Gordon, the power-driven lieutenant-governor of New Brunswick. As Christopher Moore writes in *1867: How the Fathers Made a Deal*, Gordon was "unshakeably certain that he was meant to rule New Brunswick as an Imperial potentate." Gordon assumed he would have more power if the Maritime provinces united. He was definitely not interested in a union of all the British provinces.

There were many contentious issues in any discussion of Maritime Union: Where would the capital be? Who would head that government? How would issues of commerce, schools, shipping, or trade be decided, and by whom? All these questions and more made the Maritime politicians less than keen to join their three small provinces together, and so, in a brilliant effort to be free of any blame for what could develop from any union, or discussion of a union, the politicians and parties in power made sure to also include the Opposition. It was a bipartisan approach to a singular and significant event in Canada's history, and the very bipartisan nature of the talks are what helped make Confederation successful. Moore attributes the initial bipartisan move to Charles Tupper. Delegates from all the political parties were invited to, and were part of, the Charlottetown conference. Further, the Canadians' proposal for a union of all the British provinces was welcomed as a proposition that would sideline the issue of Maritime Union. This larger union would also, later, be viewed by the Maritimers as a way to extend their influence, and Maritime issues, beyond the narrow confines of their small provinces.

Prince Edward Island would not even have participated in the talks if they hadn't been held on the Island. Living on an island, residents were self-sufficient. They didn't feel they needed anyone else; indeed, they felt that they would only lose out in any federation, or larger union. They believed that such a union would deprive them of the fruits of what they had already accomplished for themselves. This stance is made clear in an editorial from the *Islander*, June 24, 1864, reprinted in the Charlottetown *Guardian*, June 30, 2014:

> UNION OF THE COLONIES. In this Island, the newspapers generally have declared against it, and it is seldom that one meets, among our agriculturalists, a man who will listen to anything in favor of a proposition which would deprive the Colony of its existence as a separate Government.
>
> "We are very well as we are," say our farmers, "our public debt is nothing — it is not, in reality, equal to half a year's revenue. The neighboring Provinces have created

> large public debts by building Railways, why should we agree to share their indebtedness, seeing that without doing so we enjoy all the advantages of their Railroads?"

Being the smallest province, and, of course, being separated from the mainland, made it likely that the Islanders were correct about how things would go for them. And it was the railway (its creation, and its debt) that eventually "drove" Prince Edward Island into Confederation — but not till 1873.

Still, as the noted PEI historian Francis Bolger points out, there was some positive talk of the idea of a federal union on Prince Edward Island, certainly more positive than that of a Maritime Union. Nevertheless, the interest was so lackadaisical that the lieutenant-governor of PEI, George Dundas, had to be spurred on by a sudden visit from the lieutenant-governor of Nova Scotia, Richard MacDonnell, even to answer a telegram from Governor General Lord Charles Monck outlining the Canadian government's request to make a presentation at the conference. And thus, finally, Charlottetown was chosen as the location for the conference, and September 1 was set as the date for its start.

In this sultry late summer, the Maritime delegates (minus Newfoundland, which was not included at this point) convened at Charlottetown to begin their talk of Maritime Union, and to wait for the Canadians — to hear from them about the more palatable idea of a federal union.

And why would the Maritimers be interested in a federal union? In brief, there was the possibility of an intercolonial railway, and the threat of the ongoing American Civil War. The colonies (all the colonies, both from the Maritimes and Canada) worried that the expansionist mood of the States might lead its government to pursue the annexing of Canada and the Maritimes.

Why the Canadians wanted Confederation is the subject of a whole other book, or many books. In short, Canada, known then as the "United Province of Canada," which was made up of Canada East (now Quebec) and Canada West (now Ontario), was in the midst of an interminable power struggle. Each half of Canada had equal representation, an equal number of votes in Parliament, and the population and government of both sides often disagreed. The issues of Canada East — rural, French, and Catholic — were significantly different from the issues of Canada West — growing in number with its influx of immigration. The parties in power kept falling, and the United Province of Canada was at an impasse.*

The Macdonald-Taché government of Canada fell on June 14, 1864, defeated by just two votes. There had already been four elections in two years. The government was in deadlock. That's when George Brown of the Reform Party offered to form a coalition with the Macdonald-Taché government, *if* they agreed to consider representation by population through a union of the British colonies — in other words, a confederation. Historian W.L. Morton described the reaction when John A. Macdonald announced the agreement in *The Critical Years 1857–1853*:

> The House, wearied of piecemeal and sterile politics, wearied of a prolonged crisis, rose cheering, and leaders and backbenchers alike stumbled into the aisles and poured onto the floor. The leaders shook hands and clapped shoulders; with a spring the little Bleu member for Montcalm, Joseph Dufresne, embraced the tall Brown and hung from the neck of the embarrassed giant. The tension of years of frustration broke in the frantic rejoicing.

The Canadians were in far greater need of Confederation than the Maritimers, and they'd done everything in their power to get an invite to the Maritime conference. Macdonald had the governor general make the official request to the Maritimers. It was luck and coincidence that things lined up the way they did.

The other (and more exciting) cause of the indifference in Charlottetown to this historic conference was the presence of Slaymaker and Nichols' Olympic Circus, the first circus to play on the Island in twenty years. People

* This is but a brief note on the why and how Union appealed to the people of 1864 — there is much more discussion of the topic in many history books and journals. Here, as our interest is in Mercy Coles, I am including but the briefest of notes for some context on Canada's Confederation.

came from all over the colony, and even across the Northumberland Strait, from Shediac, New Brunswick, and beyond, to see the circus. The circus arrived Tuesday, August 30, and was leaving September 2. All the hotels, carriages, everything had been booked by the circus-goers, leaving the Canadians, the famous Fathers of Confederation — John A. Macdonald, George-Étienne Cartier, George Brown, D'Arcy McGee, and the others — to stay out on their ship, the *Queen Victoria*. They did have a hold full of champagne, mind you.

The lack of attention given to the arriving delegates was reported on disparagingly in all the newspapers. On September 2, the *Islander* commented this way:

> Upon arriving in Charlottetown [at noon on Thursday, September 1], Honourable W.H. Pope, Colonial Secretary, met the Delegates, but no carriages were in waiting except for a few private ones belonging to friends of one or two of the delegates. The reason why the whole duty devolved upon Mr. Pope, I have been told, was that his colleagues in the Government were all attending the circus, the feats of horsemanship, the saying and doings of Goodwin's clown … having greater attention for them than men of like position with themselves.

Of course, the *Islander* was owned by Pope himself, and so he is given credit, but this report was, in fact, true. William Pope was the only person from the PEI government to greet the Canadians, though the greeting was hardly very official-looking or formal. Because the whole town was at the circus, Pope had to have himself rowed out in a small bumboat — a boat that met arriving ships in the harbour to sell them local produce.

Pope had also gone to meet the New Brunswickers, who arrived along with Lieutenant-Governor Arthur Gordon on the *Princess of Wales*, at eleven o'clock the night before. Their rooms were at the Mansion House, while Gordon was the guest of George Dundas, PEI's lieutenant-governor. The Nova Scotians had arrived earlier in the evening of Wednesday, August 31, but weren't met. Pope reportedly found them and showed them to the Pavilion Hotel.

Under the heading "And Still They Come," the *Vindicator* reported on Wednesday, September 7:

> On Wednesday night [August 31] the *Princess of Wales* brought some 200 passengers from Shediac and Summerside.… The circus also drew a large number of persons from all parts of the Island into the City, which has never been so crowded, except during the visit of the Prince of Wales, in 1860.

And thus the party began and continued: circus, champagne, sun, and union together. George Dundas gave a dinner party that first evening for as many of the delegates as he could fit at his house. No doubt Arthur Gordon was in attendance. He left PEI soon after, probably peeved that the Canadians had taken the wind out of his desired Maritime Union sails.

In the *Guardian*'s "Extract from a Diary," Mercy Coles wrote:

> The delegates from Quebec, Halifax, and Saint John arrived in Charlottetown on August 30, 1864 and held their first meeting in the Council Chamber. Dr. Tupper came to see us and said that a party of them had had an enjoyable ride and a shoot that was more amusing than profitable. This excursion, if not immortalized [was] at least commemorated by the Island Bard, the late John LePage.

This excerpt demonstrates the difficulty with the 1917 newspaper article. The dates are wrong, and because it is told as a summary of something that happened in the past, it loses the vividness of her original diary.

On Friday, September 2, William Pope gave a large luncheon in the late afternoon consisting of Prince Edward Island delicacies: oysters, lobster — and champagne, of course. The moon was full, and it was a beautiful night. Some of the Canadians went boating, other delegates took drives or walked in the evening air. George Brown wrote that he spent the evening on Pope's balcony, "looking out at the sea in all its glory."[1]

It was the Canadians' turn on Saturday, and they gave a sumptuous luncheon on the *Queen Victoria*. The delegates ate and drank so much that the party continued until late in the evening. Brown wrote to his wife, Anne:

> Cartier and I made eloquent speeches — of course — and whether as a result of our eloquence or of the goodness of our champagne, the ice became completely broken, the tongues of the delegates wagged merrily, and the banns of matrimony between all the provinces of B.N.A having been formally proclaimed and all manner of person duly warned then and there to speak or forever after to hold their tongues — no man appeared to forbid the banns and the union was thereupon formally completed and proclaimed!

The delegates were swept up in a new and optimistic nationalist mood. The party continued that evening at a dinner held by Premier John Hamilton Gray at his estate, Inkerman House. His daughters, Margaret and Florence, helped him host at the dinner, as their mother was ill. Margaret was one of the daughters who also went to the Quebec conference.* There was a short piece, titled "She Saw Canada Born," in the *Winnipeg Free Press* on September 1, 1937, that told some of Margaret's story in Quebec.

George Coles gave a grand luncheon at Stone Park Farm on Monday, September 5. Brown was taken by the Coles women: "At four we lunched at the residence of Mr. Coles, leader of the Parliamentary opposition. He is a brewer, farmer and distiller … and gave us a handsome set out. He has a number of handsome daughters, well educated, well informed and as sharp as needles."[2]

---

* Margaret Gray wrote diaries throughout her long life, and likely kept one for 1864, but it hasn't been found. She lived to be ninety-six, and died in December 1941. The last diary in her collection is from 1937.

On Tuesday, September 6, Edward Palmer gave the luncheon, and the lieutenant-governor and his wife gave a grand ball at Government House in the evening. On Wednesday, September 7, the Canadians hosted the lieutenant-governor and his wife, and the delegates and theirs, on the *Queen Victoria*. Mercy's newspaper extract doesn't include this event, though one imagines she must have attended.

Thursday was a holiday for the delegates — from the talks, at least, though not necessarily from the festivities — and they went on excursions into the country and to PEI's warm north shore beaches. The evening held the final grand ball and banquet at Province House. There was dancing that started at ten o'clock in the assembly room, a bar and refreshments in the library, and a lavish dinner at one in the morning in the council chamber. And then the speeches began and went on for nearly three hours, even though the women were still part of the party. No doubt Mercy Coles came home very tired and "went immediately to bed," as she wrote later of other, similar occasions.

This last event, the famous "Ball and Supper," received a mishmash of odd comments in the press. Especially disparaging was the piece comparing the event to the circus.

The less-than-enthusiastic comments the Ball and Supper received after it was held matched the skeptical reception it had garnered beforehand. In the beginning, there had been such little interest in the Canadians' arrival and their proposals for union that the tickets for this last big event hadn't sold well. On September 15, *Ross's Weekly* wrote, the Ball and Supper "numerically considered was a failure; the attendance would have been a skeleton one, had not the Executive, finding at the last hour … twenty tickets only had been sold [sent free invitations to Charlottetown's elite]."

A week earlier, on the night of the banquet itself, the editor had complained how the government and its friends were attending the big ball for free, while "the citizens, Tom and Dick, and Pat, really and bonafide the givers of the Banquet and the Hop, [attended] at their own expense." The *Protestant* newspaper lambasted the circus as evil, and another retorted back that it was the Ball and Supper at which evil showed itself.

Nevertheless, the Ball and Supper, in the end, was a success. The speeches went well, if long, and the partying and drinking had continued.

The Canadians and the Maritimers went back to the *Queen Victoria* together at five o'clock, reportedly as befogged as the harbour. They were to head together to Nova Scotia and New Brunswick, but a thick mist had descended, and they waited till mid-morning to leave, no doubt a good thing for their "foggy" heads.

In contrast to the time in Prince Edward Island, with its unseasonably warm temperatures and sunny times, the conference at Quebec City involved lots of work, long hours, and incessant rain. There were still plenty of balls, dinners, and events to showcase the women; the Canadians wanted to show the Maritimers a good time in order to persuade them to join Confederation after all. The terrible weather, however, certainly affected the conference. The newspaper accounts talk of the endless rain; there was an early snowstorm when the *Queen Victoria* arrived with the rest of the Maritime delegates; and both the men and women fell sick and missed crucial discussions and the all-important events. Mercy Coles caught potentially deadly diphtheria.

*Three*

# The Journey Begins: The Lure of Travel, the New — and Leonard Tilley

Here Mercy Coles's first big journey away from home, away from Prince Edward Island and the Maritimes, starts. Here, at twenty-six years of age, Mercy would encounter the possibility of a future — of, one imagines, a desired married life, beyond the limitations of her father's home, perhaps beyond the borders of her small island. Although Mercy wouldn't be considered too old to marry, the fact that four of her seven sisters were already either married or about to be, and another was of marriageable age, would no doubt make her feel the pressure of time and opportunity, especially as she had no apparent suitors waiting for her.

As the journey starts, we have our first, and rather unexpected, romantic lead. Sir Samuel Leonard Tilley — who, his biographer C.M. Wallace in the *Dictionary of Canadian Biography* pointedly says, has been "stigmatized as a colourless druggist and temperance advocate" — was forty-six years old, and a widower of two years with seven children. He is first (and last) up.

# Reminiscences of Canada in 1864

*By Mercy Coles*

*Wednesday 5th October /64*

Left Charlottetown at 8 am. Arrived at Shediac [New Brunswick] at half past 2. I was very ill it was so rough. Monk came off in a small boat and was taken on board off Summerside. Found a special train waiting for us at Shediac, arrived at St John at 1/2 past six. Mr. Tilley and Mr. Steeves* at the Hotel to receive us. Ma, Pa, Mr. Tilley and I went to see Mrs. Perley.** Mr. Tilley did not come in.

*Thursday [October 6, 1864, Saint John, NB]*

We had a walk before breakfast and came on board *New Brunswick*. I am going to share a stateroom with Miss Alexander. Arrived at Eastport at 12, went on shore and dined, left at 1 for Portland [Maine].***

*Friday morning, [October 6], Portland, Preble House.*

We arrived here this morning after being 24 hours on board the *New Brunswick*. I went to bed at 6 and was just up in time this morning. We had an awful stormy night. We leave here in the

---

* William Steeves, a minister in Tilley's government.

** It's possible this was the widow of Moses Henry Perley, who was well-known in pre-Confederation New Brunswick as a naturalist, author, and lawyer.

*** Edward Whelan has Mrs. Alexander (whom has here been referred to as Miss Alexander) travelling to Quebec a few days later on the steamship *Queen Victoria* with most of the other Maritime delegates, though it's clear from Mercy's diary she was with Mercy's group. The erroneous information about Mrs. Alexander is not particularly crucial; it just points out how "official" recorded history can be wrong. (*The Union of the British Provinces*, 63–64)

Grand Trunk Railroad at one o'clock. We parted with Mr. Haines[*] at the wharf, he was very attentive and kind.

*Saturday, [October] 8th*

We arrived at Island Pond last night at half past 9.[**] We got up this morning at half past 4. We have just started in cars again and one might just as well try to write on horseback. We saw some beautiful scenery coming through New Hampshire, it was too dark to see the White Mountains. *Mr. Tilley helped me admire it. It is rather a joke, he is the only beau of the party and with 5 single ladies*[***] *he has something to do to keep them all in good humour* [emphasis mine].

*Saturday Afternoon, October 8, Quebec*

We arrived here yesterday at ½ past 5. There was no person there to meet us as they did not expect us to arrive for half an hour. We drove to the Russell House first. They told us the St. Louis was taken for the delegates, so we came here. I changed my dress and when I came down I found Mr. Brown in the drawing room. Mr. Bernard[****] had been in a few minutes before, in a minute Mr. Cartier, John A. Macdonald and McGee arrived. Before dinner was announced we were introduced to the Newfoundland Delegates, Mr. Shea and Mr. Carter. Mr. Cartier took Ma into dinner. John A. took Mrs. Pope. We had a splendid dinner and I enjoyed it. We had been travelling in the cars from half past 6 till half past 5. From Richmond to Somerset we only came at the rate of 9 miles an hour. A special train met us there and we came into Point Levi flying.

---

* Identity unknown.

** In the *Guardian* extract in 1917, Mercy added: "A quaint old building, the hotel was three-storied."

*** Mercy, Mrs. Alexander, the two Misses Steeves, and Jane Fisher.

**** Hewitt Bernard, secretary of the conference.

How can I describe my first impression of Quebec. It was pouring rain when we landed. We were shut up in a little cab, Ma, Miss Fisher and myself. I was in dread the whole time the horse would fall down, however he brought us here all right. It is a very nice Hotel and every comfort one can wish for. I sent Mrs. Penney a letter I had for her from Mrs. Walker.

We have been for a drive around Spencer Wood.* It is a very pretty road. You see the valley below with the River St. Charles winding along. We saw Wolfe's Monument on the Plains of Abraham and a monument to the brave who fell at the taking of Quebec, we did not go into the Cemetery as they do not admit carriages on Sunday and the snow was on the trees so thick it would not have been pleasant. We went to the Cathedral this morning. Bishop Williams preached. The music was very good, the organist played a very fine voluntary. *Pa, Ma, Mr. Tilley and I sat just together* [emphasis mine].

The steamer** has not yet arrived with the rest of the party but they expect them today. Major Bernard tells me we are to have good times. There is to be a reception on Tuesday and a Public Ball on Friday. The first word almost he said was, "I hope you brought the irresistible blue silk." I am very glad I brought the lace. Mrs. Penny has just been here, she is looking so well, she has invited Ma and I to come to see her after dinner. Mr. Galt, Mr. Cartier, Mr. Couchon, Mr. Cameron*** and a lot of other gentlemen were here at the same time. Mr. Galt gave me such a warm welcome to Canada.

---

* Spencer Wood was the home of the governors general from 1854 to 1867. The house at Spencer Wood burned down in 1860, and was rebuilt in 1863 for the new governor general, Lord Monck, who served from 1861 to 1868. Rideau Hall in Ottawa was bought and renovated by the Canadian government in 1866 to be the new residence for the governors general from 1867. The original estate was sold by the Canadian government in 1870 and is now a park, the Bois-de-Coulonge.

** The *Queen Victoria*, which the Canadians sent for the Maritime delegates.

*** Possibly Donald Cameron, whom Emma Tupper married in 1869.

Wolfe's monument, Plains of Abraham, Quebec City, 1865. Visitors kept taking pieces of the original monument. As a result, in 1849 it had to be replaced by a new column, which was surrounded by an iron fence topped with spikes to discourage souvenir hunters.

Place d'Armes and English Cathedral, Quebec City, 1860. This is Cathedral of the Holy Trinity, where "Bishop Williams preached" on Sunday, October 9, 1864. It was constructed in 1804, and was the first Anglican cathedral to be built outside the British Isles.

Basilica of Notre Dame de Québec, Quebec City, 1859. Mercy Coles referred to the Cathedral-Basilica of Notre-Dame de Québec as the "French Cathedral." The Cathedral of the Holy Trinity, which she and her family attended while in Quebec, was often called the "English Cathedral" by the people in Quebec City. This reflected the ethnicity of the parishioners who attended, since the English were more likely to be Protestant, while the French were more likely to be Roman Catholic.

*Monday morning, October 10*

The Steamer arrived last night with the rest of the delegates. Such a Babel when they came in. The two Misses Gray* Mrs. and Miss [Emma] Tupper, Mrs. and Miss [Joanna] Archibald are the ladies. All the gentlemen are gone to the Conference. Mr. McDougall brought his daughter [Jessie] to see me and we went out shopping together. I bought an Opera Cloak. Paid 8 ½ dollars** for it. It is very pretty. I am sewing the trimming on my velvet jacket. Dr. Tupper and Mr. Henry called to see Eliza*** when they were at Ch'Town. Mr. Whelan is here, we are going to luncheon. After luncheon Mr. Drinkwater**** called and he, Ma and I went for a drive. We went to see the French Cathedral, then we went to see the Seminary Chapel where all the fine paintings are. We drove round the Battery and then went to the Province Building to see the Library. We met Mr. Bernard in the hall, he introduced us to the sergeant-at-arms and the Clerk of the House [Mr. Lea]. The Library is nothing very wonderful. When we came back Mrs. Campbell the wife of the Hon. Mr. Campbell lunched with us.

When the gentlemen came from Conference they brought cards of invitation to Mrs. and Miss Tupper, Miss Gray and Mrs. Alexander to dine at Gov't House. Ma and I have a card for Wednesday. I wonder Mrs. Pope was not invited before Mrs. Alexander? We made a kind of acquaintance with the organist at the Cathedral, Mr. Peirce. Mr. McDougall and his daughter dined with us. Papa and all the gentlemen who were not dining at Gov't House were dining at the Strathcona Club.*****

---

* Margaret, daughter of Colonel Gray of PEI, and Charlotte Elizabeth, the daughter of Colonel Gray of Saint John, NB.

** According to the Bank of Canada, this would equal about $230 in 2010 dollars.

*** Mercy's younger sister, who would have been the eldest sister at home while Mercy and her parents were away.

**** Charles Drinkwater, John A. Macdonald's secretary.

***** This was probably the Stadacona Club.

Mr. Drinkwater has promised to get me a bouquet for tomorrow night. It will be rather a stupid affair tomorrow night, so they say.

*Wednesday morning, October 12*

We all went to the Drawing Room last night* quite a crowd when we all got together, all the ladies looked very well and were quite a credit to the Lower Provinces.** Pa, Ma and I went together. A half dozen gentlemen wanted to take me into the room but I preferred to go in with Papa. The Governor General stood in the middle with his Private Secretary on his right hand. We did not require to have any cards. The Aides announced us each in turn. The Governor shook hands very friendly with each one. After all those who had the privilege of entrée were presented they formed a half circle, the rest of the people then walked in at one door, bowed to the Governor and passed out at the other. There were about 800 people presented and I was very tired before it was all over. *Mr. Tilley took charge of me and walked about with me the whole evening* [emphasis mine]. When we came home Ma and I went immediately to bed we were so tired. Ma wore her grenadine over black silk. I wore my blue silk. There were only 2 or 3 trains there.

It was not only Mercy who found Leonard Tilley attractive and worthy of romantic interest. Tilley, as Moore writes in his seminal book on Confederation, *1867: How the Fathers Made a Deal,* "has dropped almost completely off the radar screen of Canadian history." In the 1930s historian W.M. Whitelaw noted that the little written on Tilley was "particularly distressing."[1] Leonard Tilley definitely bears a closer examination. Who was he? What was he like? And why were Mercy and Mrs. Alexander, at the very least,

---

* Held at the parliament buildings and given by the governor general, Lord Monck.

** The Lower Provinces are the Maritime provinces.

Sir Samuel Leonard Tilley, October 29, 1864. Tilley was supposed to accompany Mercy to have her photo taken, but Mercy notes that she missed this opportunity because she "was not punctual." He went on ahead, and had his photograph done earlier that day, along with Emma Tupper and her mother, among others.

attracted to him? Tilley was just forty-six years old in 1864, and had been widowed two and a half years earlier. He had seven children, five of whom were still young. He was known for his good head and grasp of finances, not his charms. However, Mercy Coles's comments provide us with new insight into Leonard Tilley, the man.

Known to history as Sir Samuel Leonard Tilley, though he never used his first name, Leonard Tilley was born in 1818 in Gagetown, New Brunswick. He married at twenty-five, and was widowed by forty-four. His wife, Julia, died of cancer, and he'd been hit hard by her loss. His friend, the politician Joseph Howe, of Nova Scotia, recommended "[u]nremitting, anxious, hard-driven work."

Now, in October 1864, we find him on his way to Quebec, happily playing the role of "the only beau … with five single ladies to look after." Mercy writes of him spending his time with her, and also with Mrs. Alexander, the forty-year-old widowed sister of the PEI politician Thomas Haviland. These two were the oldest single women along for the Confederation conferences. It may be that he enjoyed the company of more mature women, or it may be that he was thinking of his five young motherless children still at home, and thought that Mercy or Mrs. Alexander seemed like the most viable options for his attention.

There isn't much written about Leonard Tilley. Hardly anyone, it seems, has found him or his life interesting enough to examine, which is strange, as, at the very least, he was the premier of New Brunswick pre-Confederation, in federal politics post-Confederation, and lived through politically lively times. Mercy's writings on Tilley offer a chance to give him a second look.

The view of Tilley that persists in history is not one of a visionary; he didn't dream big. He was a storekeeper, a businessman, a bean-counter; in short, he was boring. But that can't be the full story.

Physically, he was slight and clean-shaven. Neither John A. Macdonald or Tilley had beards, moustaches, or the facial hair common in the 1860s — odd-looking to us today — the mutton chop sideburns that reach around and extend under the chin in a scraggly fashion. He was rosy-cheeked, and had an easy smile — one he often flashed. He was considered agreeable, friendly, and intelligent — attractive qualities that made him quite pleasant to be around.

He also had an excellent head for finances, and dominated the New Brunswick legislature with his ability to argue his points. At the Confederation conference in Quebec City, he won extra money for New Brunswick during the discussion of the financial resolutions, which was one of the things that really peeved the Prince Edward Island delegates. During the Quebec conference, as Wallace points out in his biography of Tilley, a *Montreal Gazette* reporter said of him, "Any ordinary man can open an argument, most men can keep it up, but Mr. Tilley always knows where the matter ends." Such persistence and persuasiveness are, of course, always good traits when courting.

Tilley created the National Policy on tariffs and trade (to encourage and protect industry and the economy) in 1879; this policy would go on to form the basis for Canada's trade policy for years. Speaking of the creation of a federation of the separate provinces and the railway that could bring it together, he remarked, "Statesmen … should try 'to bind together the Atlantic and Pacific by a continuous chain of settlements and line of communications *for that [is] the destiny of this country, and the race which inhabits it*'"[2] [emphasis mine]. In March 1879, commenting on the National Policy, he said, "The time has arrived when we are to decide whether we will be simply hewers of wood and drawers of water … *or will rise to the position, which, I believe Providence has destined us to occupy*" [emphasis mine]. Progress, humanity, destiny — these are all words aimed to inspire and they show the ability to dream. They reveal at least some degree of passion, even if Tilley himself is little remembered by history.

Tilley entered politics in 1850, and had been involved in the railway and advocating for prohibition in New Brunswick since 1844. He remained in office till 1893, spending the last eight years as lieutenant-governor of New Brunswick. He died in June 1896, still writing political treatises. Fifty years in politics is no small feat. One could argue he was a visionary, and had passion — and the persistence to continue the fight to get the best for the people he represented. He had to have had presence and leadership to last fifty years. Wallace says Tilley wasn't widely popular, that he didn't have John A. Macdonald's flair or earthiness. No doubt that's true, but it is an unfair comparison. What politician has achieved the fame, or had the flair, of John A.? The closest one would be Pierre Trudeau, and that's a different story altogether.

Tilley loved politics. He stayed with it through thick and thin. He remained when his political colleagues had given up on him (when New Brunswickers voted against him and against Confederation in the big election of 1865); and he remained when he was frustrated at his lack of power, not getting the minister of finance position he wanted, and likely deserved, in Macdonald's first government of 1867 (Alexander Galt was granted the portfolio). Tilley did ask to leave in 1871, after his father's death, partly because it seemed he didn't expect to be given the finance portfolio, even though Galt had left. Tilley did, however, stay on, and finally got the position in 1873. When in power, he didn't back down, even when his bills met with violent opposition. For example, when Tilley's prohibition bill was passed in New Brunswick in January 1856, it was so unpopular he was burned in effigy, his house was attacked, and there were threats to his life. Through it all, he stayed.

Persistent, passionate, persuasive, as well as intelligent, attractive, friendly, and genial, Tilley must have been putting all these skills to work in his courtship of at least two of the women at the Confederation conference, as Mercy notes both she and Mrs. Alexander received his attention. He was still youngish, yet he was old enough to have a maturity women find attractive. He also possessed the aphrodisiac of power, even if he didn't have John A.'s level of charisma. And, of course, he was a Maritimer to boot. For Mercy Coles and the other women, what was there not to like?

*Four*

# From the Sublime to the Ridiculous: The "Failed," the Grand Success, or the Drunken Fiasco of the Government Ball

*Thursday, October 13 to Monday, October 17*

It's lucky we have Mercy's diary. If we were to consider only the previously collected documents having to do with Confederation, all of which are from men's perspectives, we would be left with a very different take on the conference's events. In this first week of the conference, Mercy writes of D'Arcy McGee's drunkenness, and of the terrible weather in Quebec City. McGee was known for his earthiness, like John A. Macdonald, and for his punning. He must have said or done something to "make her take no notice of him" at their dinner at Spencer Wood. One wonders what it was. She notes that the famous British journalist George Augustus Sala dined with them, though she was "rather disappointed in the man…."

From this first week we get a sense of what Mercy would have taken note of and how she would have written about people and events had she not fallen ill with diphtheria at the end of the week. The Nova Scotian delegate Charles Tupper was a medical doctor who always carried his black medical bag with him, and he attended to Mercy during her illness and recuperation. Mercy was not isolated from the others, though. She heard about the events and balls she missed from the other young women, and had a number of visitors, including Leonard Tilley and some of the other men who may have been courting her.

Despite the fact that her direct observation of events was somewhat limited, Mercy was still able to offer considerable insight into the goings-on at the conference, and the characters of and relationships among the people there. The comparison between what has been written and published officially and Mercy's writings allows us a different view of the events of Confederation.

Lorette Falls, from below the falls looking up, near Montmorency, about 1860.

*Thursday morning, October 13, Quebec City*
Yesterday we went to see the falls of Lorette and the Indian Chief. It was raining and we could not walk down the gorge, just stood on the bridge and saw the waterfall. Col. Gray PEI chaperoned the party. We had Mr. Crowther, Mr. Galt's secretary in the carriage with Miss [Jessie] McDougall, Ma and I. We went to the Indian Chief's house. Not at all what I expected to see, the only sign of it being Indian was a Tomahawk and Chief's cap which they showed us. I bought a wooden spoon to take home as a curiosity. The Old Chief is the last of the Huron Tribe. His wife, an old woman 90 years of age was sitting alongside of him. He has two silver armlets presented by George IV and a medal by the Prince of Wales. In the evening we dined at the Governor General's, it was a very pleasant party.* *D'Arcy McGee took me to dinner and sat between Lady MacDonnell and I. Before dinner was half over he got so drunk he was obliged to leave the table. I took no notice of him. Mr. Gray said I acted admirably* [emphasis mine].** The sun has not shone for two hours ever since we have been here. I was never in such a place.

---

* Edward Whelan obviously thought it was a pleasant party, too. He wrote:

> I have just returned (11 o'clock, p.m.) from dining at Spencer Wood, the residence of the Governor General. It is hardly necessary to say that the dinner was a superb one — lacking nothing in the departments of cuisine and vintage; but rendered especially charming by the ease, affability and good humour which characterized the intercourse of the numerous guests; which included many of the Delegates, several of the Canadian Ministry; and last, but not least, several of the fair daughters of different parts of Canada, one or two of whom I should like to particularize, but dare not. ("Edward Whelan Reports from the Quebec Conference," ed. Peter B. Waite, *Canadian Historical Review* XLII [1961])

** In the June 1917 extract from her diary, Mercy leaves out the part about D'Arcy McGee getting drunk and having to leave the table, as well as her comments on the weather and Quebec City.

*Friday morning, October 14, Quebec City*
Raining again. Will it ever be fine? Sala* dined with us last night. I was rather disappointed in the man, a rough new faced Englishman. Black eyes and hair and such a red nose and face. Mr. Brown sat alongside of him and introduced him to me. I have a sore throat this morning. Col Gray has given me some Homeopathic medicine. I hope it will cure. We want to make some visits today.

I have written a long letter to Eliza. The Governor's Ball is to come off tonight. They say it's going to be such a crush. Mother and I went for a walk on Durham Terrace.** While there a large piece of rock fell. When the men came in they said a baby was killed.

This additional comment can be found in her extract in the *Guardian*, June 30, 1917:

> At first we thought the house nearby was on fire owing to the great amount of dust that arose. When the gentlemen came home from the Conference they said that the rock had pierced the roof of the house and killed a child in a cradle.

*Monday afternoon — 17, Quebec City*
Home all alone. I have not been able to leave my bedroom since Friday. Just as I was going to get ready for the Ball I went to comb Mamma's hair and nearly fainted. She made me lie down. I got so nervous and excited that I commenced crying. Papa went off for

---

* George Augustus Sala was a famous British journalist, who was travelling through Canada and the United States in 1864. He was in Quebec City as a correspondent for the *Daily Telegraph.*

** Durham Terrace, which is the terrace and boardwalk in front of the Château Frontenac, was renamed Dufferin Terrace in 1879. It was originally built in 1838, and extended in 1854.

Dr. Tupper,* he came up directly. He wrote some prescriptions and sent them off to have some medicine made up for me. He saw I had a very sore throat and was very feverish, of course going to the Ball was out of the question so I very soon undressed and got into bed. Mrs. Penny came in to see us dressed and kindly offered to stay with me while Mamma was at the ball. They did not start until nearly 11 o'clock and were home by 2. Dr. Tupper came in again when he came home. He saw I was very ill indeed. All day Saturday I never raised my head from the pillow, only to take the medicine or gargle my throat. Yesterday morning it broke, it still remains very sore. The Doctor has just been here and he says I shall be quite well in a few days. I hope so for there are two or three Balls and parties this week, one "at Home" at Government House on Friday night and a party at Madame Tessier's** on Wednesday.

Papa and Ma have gone out to make some visits. Mr. Crowther has just called and left a comic newspaper for me with his compliments. He, Mr. Drinkwater, and Mr. Bernard call every day to enquire for me. *The Ball*** I believe was rather a failure as far as the delegates are concerned. The Quebec people never introduced the ladies nor gentlemen to any partners nor never seen whether they had any supper or not* [emphasis mine]. The Col Grays**** are both rather indignant at the way their daughters were treated. Miss [Margaret] Gray and Miss Tupper came to see me this morning. They came to the conclusion I had not missed much yet. They all went to

---

* It's been suggested that Charles Tupper quite enjoyed his tending to the wives and daughters of his colleagues, though Mercy's accounts of him don't lead one to conclude anything untoward happened with her.

** Wife of Ulric-Joseph Tessier, the speaker of the legislative assembly of the Province of Canada.

*** The Ball was held at the parliament buildings by the Canadian government for the Maritime delegates on Friday October 14.

**** Col. John Hamilton Gray, premier of PEI, and Col. John Hamilton Gray, a lawyer and former premier of New Brunswick.

The Citadel, with the Wolfe and Montcalm Monument, Quebec City, about 1860. This image also provides a good view of the rock cliffs, where rock slides often happened after heavy rains. The Wolfe and Montcalm Monument is different from the Wolfe Monument on the Plains of Abraham. The monument in this photograph was erected in 1827 by Governor General Lord Dalhousie, in the Governor's Garden, to pay tribute to both of the generals, who died in September 1759.

> Montmorency [Falls] Saturday. The only gentleman with them Mr. Livesay* and he rode on the box.

Here is where history gets interesting. Luckily, even though Mercy was away sick, she kept on top of all the goings-on, concerned about what she was missing. Because of that, we get to see what was really happening — the social culture that helped make (or not make, in PEI's case) the important relationships that mattered for Confederation.

Along with Mercy's writing, we have the record of another woman who helped to document the social side of the conference events.

Frances Elizabeth Owen Cole Monck, known as Feo to her family, was the sister-in-law of Lord Monck. She was married to his brother Richard, the governor general's private secretary. Feo was also the niece of Lord Monck, as she was the daughter of Lady Monck's eldest sister. Feo travelled to Canada in May 1864, and remained till May 1865. While here, she kept a journal. It is lively and full of details of life at Spencer Wood, her travels around the country, and the social side of the political events and people shaping Canada at that time. The journal is made up of a collection of letters that were sent back home and meant to inform and entertain her family. In her letters, she describes the beauty of the scenery around her, and also makes fun of herself, her husband, the people around her, the customs of her time and place, and the delegates at the Quebec conference.

Feo had a very different social status and background from Mercy Coles. These helped to shape her views. She was also privy to more information about, and had more exposure to, the politicians of the time, because of living at Spencer Wood, and her close proximity to the governor general. When Lady Monck, Lord Monck's wife, returned to Ireland with their children for the fall and winter of 1864–65, Feo took her place as the mistress of the house, serving as hostess at the many dinners held by Lord Monck.

---

* Livesay was an older man, involved with the railway, and was probably the "Cockney fop … dogging the steps of the Delegation through the Provinces" described by Edward Whelan.

Lady Frances Elizabeth Owen Cole Monck, known as Feo to her family.

A version of Feo's journal was published in 1891 as *My Canadian Leaves*, but the far more telling and interesting unedited version of her journal, compiled and annotated by W.L. Morton and included in *Monck Letters and Journals, 1863–1868: Canada from Government House at Confederation*, was published in 1970. It is full of juicy notes and gossip one doesn't find anywhere else.

Mercy's and Feo's writings show how limited our understanding of the social history of Confederation would be if we weren't able to examine what they had to say about the people and events of the time. Mercy's view is one take on the Ball; Edward Whelan, who was a pro-Confederation delegate from Prince Edward Island, provides another, very different view; and Feo Monck has yet another take.

Edward Whelan, in his *The Union of the British Provinces,* says:

> On the evening of the 14th a very brilliant Ball was given in the Parliament Buildings, under the auspices of the Canadian Ministry. It was attended by the same classes — the same distinguished persons and society as attended the "Drawing Room" on the 11th. [In contrast, Mercy thought this was quite tiresome.] His Excellency the Governor General, His Excellency the Lieut. Governor of Nova Scotia [Sir Richard MacDonnell] and Lady, the Members of the Canadian Government, the Delegates from the Eastern Provinces, and about 800 others, formed a large and most agreeable party, by whom the pleasures of the dance were kept up without interruption and *without an incident to mar the harmony of the occasion* [emphasis mine], until nearly 3 o'clock on the morning of the 15th.[1]

Feo Monck, in her journal on October 16, provides a description given by her cousin, F. Burrows, who claims the event was "most amusing; such drunkenness, pushing, kicking and tearing, he says, he never saw; his own coattails were nearly torn off; the supper room floor was covered with meat, drink, and broken bottles."

Feo Monck's own description of the ball is here. Note that the / / surround the parts that were cut out of her diary in the edited version, *My Canadian Leaves.*

> October 15, Saturday
> The G-G then introduced me to Sir Robert Macdonnell [*sic*].* He asked me to walk about with him and have some refreshments, so off we went.... Well this old king and I wandered on and on for a long time, him being too grand to ask the way.... I wonder how they could entrust any government to him!... [A]nd when we at last found the right room, I danced with Dr. Tupper / who trembled with nervousness as I whirled him through the Lancers.... I am making so many blunders but my head aches and these delegates puzzle me so/.

Whelan's account of the ball in his *Examiner* is a bit more forthcoming than in his later *Union of the British Provinces.*

> It was a stunning and crushing affair as regards numbers, gorgeous dress, lavish expenditure on the part of the Government: and, indeed, everything that was calculated to make a sensational sacrifice at the shrine of pleasure. I do not think the arrangements were quite so good and regular as they were at our small Ball in Charlottetown when the Delegates met there. There, the Delegates from the other Provinces were introduced to our Society, such as it is, by persons appointed for the purpose. Here, the Delegates from the Maritime Provinces — (and I speak of the whole of introduction to the Quebec belles and gentlemen, Those

* Richard MacDonnel was lieutenant-governor of Nova Scotia, 1864–65. In the end, he was moved out of the position because he didn't support the idea of Confederation. The job was given to Sir Fenwick Williams, of whom Mercy writes later.

> who brought ladies from the Lower Provinces had to do, for the most part, the cicerone business themselves: and it was not pleasant to see the lady of the Provincial Secretary of Nova Scotia [Mrs. Charles Tupper] — a very fine and handsome woman — led to the Supper Room by an antiquated, grey-headed Cockney fop, without influence or position, and who seems to be dogging the steps of the Delegation through the Provinces. However, I will say nothing more upon this point. The Canadian Ministry, I am sure, were desirous of making the entertainment as agreeable as possible to their guests: and if any error were committed, it was not of the heart but of the head.

Whelan did not wish to be critical; in fact, he wanted to impress. His book *Union of the British Provinces* was compiled after the fact, after the conferences had ended and the delegates had had the opportunity to edit and revise their speeches. His aim was to sell the idea of Confederation to the people through what must, to some extent, be seen as propaganda. He published the book with his own money in Charlottetown in 1865; he made hardly any of it back, however, as much of Prince Edward Island's population had turned decidedly against the idea of Confederation by that time.

*Five*

# Diphtheria

While in Quebec City, Mercy Coles fell sick with diphtheria. At the time, diphtheria was a serious concern, and was often fatal. She was so ill that she ended up missing most of the events in Quebec City, where the conference continued until October 26. One benefit of her absence and illness, however, was that they brought her more attention from many of the men. This was certainly some consolation for her, but couldn't make up for her lost opportunities both to woo and be wooed.

At the time, there was no cure for diphtheria. There were, however, some rather dramatic treatments for the symptoms, and Mercy had to endure some of both: the treatments, and the symptoms. Despite her illness, however, she was not isolated from what was going on. People at the time had little idea of how diseases were transmitted, and so the highly contagious Mercy had many visits from the other young women, and from a number of the delegates and secretaries, including Leonard Tilley, Hewitt Bernard, and Charles Drinkwater.

*Tuesday Afternoon, October 18, Quebec City*
I am sure I shall know the shape of every shingle on the roof of the old house opposite. I went downstairs for about a half an hour in the middle of the day. I felt very weak and was very glad to come back to my bedroom again. I saw a few of the guests however, I think they had not all returned. While I was there the servant brought in invitations from the Bachelors of Quebec to a Ball at the Provincial Building on Friday evening. We are also invited to a party tomorrow evening. I hope I shall be able to go. My throat does not seem much improved, the other side is very painful. Mrs. Tupper said at first it was Diphtheria. I fancied so from the medicine and wine I had to take. I have not seen the Doctor since morning. I then told him he need not come. I should be downstairs but I could not wait for him, the talking made my head ache. They have all gone to see the Citadel. I shall have to miss all the sights. Never mind, I feel I shall get quite well whenever we leave Quebec. *It's the most miserable place to live in one can fancy. We have not had one fine day ever since we came. It has been pouring just a few minutes ago. Such dumpy, draggled frail women they have here* [emphasis mine]. I have just seen one go by with a handsome embroidered skirt over a red one, her white one an inch thick with mud. Ma is going to have a new black silk waist made. She has only the one evening dress and finds it rather awkward.

*Wednesday Afternoon, October 19, Quebec City*
In bed again the whole day. My throat got so bad they were all frightened about it. Dr. Tupper came and opened it again. I had to hold ice in my mouth all night. This morning it is better, but the Doctor says I am not to get up today. Pa, and Ma have gone to visit the Ursuline Convent.

Mercy had a good chance of dying there in Quebec. Today, we're immunized against diphtheria, but in 1864, the incidence of the disease and the fatality rate in Canada, and around the world, were high.

The symptoms of diphtheria are a sore throat, fever, and chills — symptoms of which Mercy complains in her diary. In severe cases, a thick, grey membrane grows across the throat or mouth or the back of the nose. People die from suffocation, paralysis, and heart failure. Even with today's treatments, the fatality rate is between 5 and 10 percent.

The sore throat and development of the membrane are the immediate result of infection by the bacteria that cause the disease, and the membrane can be so thick and pervasive it can cause suffocation. The toxin secreted by the bacteria can cause problems in the rest of the body, such as heart failure and nerve damage. It was only with the discovery of the toxin, and then the antitoxin, in the 1880s and 1890s that there was a way to treat diphtheria.

In 1864, people didn't know how most diseases were caused or transmitted. The realization of the importance of sanitation and hygiene was relatively new at the time, and, although Louis Pasteur was in the process of providing solid proof for the germ origin of disease, the theory that germs could cause disease wasn't widely accepted. Indeed, it would be the early twentieth century before the general public came to accept the discoveries of Pasteur and Robert Koch, although the diphtheria bacteria had been identified in 1883, and the antitoxin, which could help neutralize the toxin, was identified in 1891 by Emil von Behring.

Epidemics of typhoid, typhus, cholera, and diphtheria were still common in Mercy Coles's time, with frequent outbreaks arising in North America, partly as a result of massive immigration to the continent from Europe. The mortality rate was high. Diphtheria was the main cause of death in children before 1900, and even until 1920 there were twelve thousand cases, and one thousand deaths, in Canada every year.

In the 1860s, the cause of diphtheria wasn't known. Some people thought it was a parasite; others were unclear whether it was, indeed, a unique disease, or was perhaps a variant of other diseases, like scarlet fever or whooping cough. And, of course, no one realized that it was contagious. Since that was the case, Mercy had visits every day from some of the delegates, and the other young women. It is little surprise, then, to learn that a number of the visitors to Quebec became sick. Dr. Tupper's daughter, Emma, was thought to have diphtheria; Mrs. Tupper was sick with a cold; and Colonel Gray of PEI said his voice was hoarse from a bad cold. Gray,

William Pope, D'Arcy McGee, and others were absent from the conference proceedings a number of times because of "indisposition."

The others may have suffered a little, but it was Mercy who had the worst time of it in Quebec City. Mercy's description of the doctor "opening" her throat is evidence of the fact that the membrane blocking it had grown so thick that it needed to be cut in order for her to breathe. She also notes that it later needed to be opened "again." She was treated with caustic ammonia and "black drafts" to dissolve the membrane. Ice was applied to soothe the inflamed tissues and take the swelling down.

As a result of her illness, Mercy missed most of the sightseeing in Quebec City. She was half-dead from diphtheria, and from having to suffer through the treatments for it — in those days, if the disease didn't kill you, the cure might. And there she was — twenty-six, and wanting to be out and about. All those parties, balls, sightseeing, and events; she was missing out on the chance of a lifetime.

There's no doubt Mercy enjoyed the special attention she received from the delegates and her suitors, however — the gifts, the special enquiries, the notes of condolence. On the one hand, she was missing the balls and the sights; on the other, she was receiving all kinds of extra attention, which made her stand out among the other young women.

Nevertheless, reading Mercy's diary, one longs, with Mercy, for better weather, to get away from Quebec, for the opportunity to go to the dances, to finally get out into the world again. Two weeks of being sick when you're young is hard enough, but missing two weeks right then, when everything was happening, and people were caught up in the excitement of the possibilities of Confederation — of becoming a bigger, stronger country — was really hard. After all, Confederation had been bandied about for years, with no real movement, and now that it was happening, the events were big. The time really was something special. From our vantage point, looking back at the important and seminal events of Quebec, one can't help but feel sympathy for Mercy and her lost opportunities.

# *Six*

# The Temptation of John A. Macdonald

*Thursday, October 20 to Wednesday, October 26*

Falling ill with diphtheria and missing all the events were not the only things Mercy had to contend with. Mercy and the other young women in Quebec knew, of course, that the affairs of their fathers would affect their own fates — their matrimonial chances, and choices. Historians have tended to dismiss Mercy as not having taken any notice of the political goings-on around her. Mercy may have intentionally disregarded the politics at times, or been knowingly oblivious to them at other points, focused as she was on her desire for something — anything — to happen, but she certainly would have known that the politics that affected her father also affected her own position. In this next week of her diary, Mercy Coles writes of John A. Macdonald, and his attentions to her, a number of times.

*Thursday Morning, October 20, Quebec City*

In bed yet. Dr. Tupper says if I lie in bed today I shall be quite well tomorrow. I hope to be able to go to church on Sunday. They had a great Ball last night at Madame Tessier's. Papa came home with every stitch of clothes wringing wet with perspiration. He says he never had such a time, the French ladies are the very mischief for flying round. John A. and he saw Madame Duval* and her daughter home. Mrs. Alexander chaperoned the young ladies. Ma, Mrs. Tupper nor Miss Archibald did not go. They had only one Island lady there, Mrs. Alexander. Miss [Margaret] Gray nor I was not able to go. Ma has just gone out, she has had a nice waist made for her black silk dress. It is a very fine day, such a pity I shall miss all the sights.

*Friday Afternoon, October 21*

Not down stairs yet. I feel a great deal better but Dr. Tupper said this morning he thought I had better not venture out of this room today. He came in and found me out of bed standing in my bare feet. Get into bed this minute he said, you want to catch your death of cold. I tumbled in pretty quickly, he felt my pulse and looked into my mouth and said you are a good deal better you soon will be well and asked me for the bottle of Caustic. I asked who was ill. He said it was Emma, his daughter. She was very poorly all night and has a little sore throat today, not nearly as bad as mine but still enough to make them very anxious. They lost a darling child about a year ago with Diphtheria.**

---

* Madame Duval was the wife of Justice Jean-François-Joseph Duval, Court of Queen's Bench, Canada East.

** From the Charlottetown *Guardian*, June 30, 1917: "The Doctor showed me a photograph of his daughter who had died of diphtheria. She was a lovely child and he felt for her death very much." This meant that Emma was his only daughter — whom he later travelled across the prairies in December of 1869 to "rescue" from Louis Riel during the Red River Rebellion.

I have had Mr. Lea [clerk of the council] to pay me a visit, the first gentleman. He was so glad to find me better. I hope I shall be able to go to church on Sunday. I have not the slightest inclination to go to the Ball tonight.* I am going to ask the Dr. to let me go down to dinner. I can put on my shawl and the dining-room is always warm. Pa and Ma have gone off to the Montmorency Falls.

*Saturday Afternoon, October 22, Quebec City*

I have been down stairs to luncheon and am going to dinner. My throat is quite well, only a little weak. The Ball was a grand affair last night. Pa and Ma went. I remained up until after they went. The Conference did not meet until 12 today and adjourns at 6. Dr. Tupper came in to see me before he went away. He says I shall be able to go out tomorrow. Ma has been out and bought me such a nice warm wrap for my neck. I went into the St. John Room yesterday. Mr. Tilley was there. He gave me such a nice carte [photograph] of himself, all the gentlemen have been having their likenesses taken. Papa's is only tolerable. I believe we are positively to leave here on Wednesday. I am heartily sick of Quebec.

John A. was making very kind enquiries about me last night, he told Ma he could not express how sorry he felt at my being ill. Mr. Livesay sent me a very kind message to day by Miss Steeves. He said he was very fond of me and was so sorry that I was ill.

*Monday afternoon, 24th*

I did not go out yesterday after all. Dr. Tupper said my throat was not well enough and indeed my own feelings were not much like going out. I laid on the sofa in the St. John Room all the time they were away at Church. Pa and Ma went to call on Mrs. [Gingras] in the afternoon. I had a visit here from Mr. Tilley, Mr.

* This was the Bachelors' Ball, held at the parliament buildings.

Bernard was up for a few minutes just as I was dressing for dinner. Mr. J.A. Macdonald dined with us last night. After dinner he entertained me with any amount of small talk, when I came to bed at 9 o'clock he said he was just going to a party at Madame Duval's. She always gives parties Sunday. This morning I went for a drive. We remained out nearly an hour. This afternoon I have been making visits with Pa and Ma. We did not go in any place but Mrs. Roy's at the Manse Hospital. She is a very pretty woman. She gave me her own and her husband's carte. Mr. McDougall sent me his today.

Another detail from this day is offered in the extract from the *Guardian*:

> [H]e [Macdonald] entertained me with small talk and gave me a conundrum,* "Why were he and Mrs. Alexander like two Roman generals?" The answer was, "She's Alexander and I sees her (Caesar)." On the following morning I went out for a drive and remained out an hour.

The following day, Mercy's diary relates more about her condition, and what it is causing her to miss.

*Tuesday Afternoon, October 25, Quebec City*
I was so ill last evening after my drive I was obliged to go to bed. I did not feel so low since I have been ill. Dr. Tupper came in to see me. I had a black draft and felt better after it was all over. *Mr. Bernard came to dinner. I was so disappointed when Ma told me* [emphasis mine]. He sent me his carte this morning. Mr. Livesay has just given me his. His white hair looks so venerable. I shall

* This discussion, on Sunday, October 23, was the first occasion when Mercy references a conundrum to do with Macdonald. It was clearly a riddle. The second instance is on October 26, and that reference does not appear to allude to a riddle.

have quite a collection for every one of the gentlemen have had theirs taken.*

Pa wrote to Tom this morning and I sent one of his. Ma and I wrote to Eliza and sent her one of Mamma's. It is very good. If I feel much better when I get to Montreal I will have mine taken. I feel much stronger this afternoon. I laid down for an hour after luncheon. I had some raw apples, the first thing I have enjoyed since I have been ill.

The Misses Steeves seem to be the possessors of the parlour down stairs. I think they never leave it. There is a Mr. Carver who seems to be the great attraction. He is a beau of Miss [Jane] Fisher's but they monopolize him. We are positively to start for Montreal on Thursday.

*Wednesday, October 26, Quebec City*

We went for a drive today. We went through the Lower Town to see where the rock fell and crushed the people to death [on Friday, October 14].** I was going out again after lunch but the carriage was so long in coming I got tired waiting and took my things off again.

---

* Presumably it was Livernois, in Quebec City, taking the photographs of the delegates and of the wives and daughters. Livernois was one of the well-known photographers in Quebec then, and he did take some of the group photos of the Fathers preserved by Library and Archives Canada (LAC). No photographs of the women have been discovered yet, but presumably he also took theirs, as Mercy writes that her mother had hers done. Likely, the other women did, too, as Mercy noted she would have hers done in Montreal if she could. Sadly, the full collection of Livernois's photographs has not been preserved, as William Notman's in Montreal was by the McCord Museum. Still, somewhere, perhaps in the keeping of the descendants of the "Daughters" of Confederation, there may yet be discovered the photographs of the young women who went to Quebec.

** Though Mercy doesn't say much about this rock slide, four people were killed; not the baby she'd heard of, but two children, and the parents of one. The newspapers made a lot of it, but the delegates didn't make any public comments on it.

> I went to dinner in the evening. John A. sat alongside of me. What an old Humbug he is.* He brought me my dessert into the Drawing Room. The conundrum.

Just as the women knew that political affairs affected them, the delegates also knew full well that how they treated the women of the conference — the wives, daughters, and unmarried sisters — would affect their desired course of events, too. As Whelan wrote, the "inveterate dancers" not missing a dance, "know[ing] if they can dance themselves into the affections of the wives and daughters of the country, the men will certainly become an easy conquest,"[1] tells us that the men acted with intention, too.

John A. Macdonald was known for his charisma and charm, for his skills of persuasion, as well as his conviviality and ease with women. And Mercy received her fair share of attention from him. That George Coles should receive Macdonald's attention isn't surprising, as PEI, though not as necessary to Confederation as New Brunswick or Nova Scotia, was still important enough for the Canadians to want it. As the conference progressed, PEI voted no over and over again to the resolutions put forward. They were often the only province to do so.

On the eve of Wednesday, October 19, the Prince Edward Island delegates were split in their opinions regarding the "rep-by-pop" basis of the conference. George Coles was of the opinion that rep-by-pop had been agreed upon in Charlottetown as the only way to proceed with Confederation. PEI's premier, Colonel Gray, was clear on that, too, but his attorney general, Edward Palmer, disagreed, as did Thomas Haviland. William Pope wasn't there that evening. The PEI delegates went off to discuss the matter among themselves, and agreed to vote in the morning. Thus, on the evening of October 19, at the party at Madame Tessier's, George Coles was in a position to sway the other PEI delegates to vote in favour of the Canadians'

* An "old humbug" in 1864 referred to someone who teased and tried to hoodwink or fool others — but in a way so flagrant that the truth was obvious. Macdonald was known to be a great teaser and player of tricks. He must have been having fun at dinner, which Mercy is commenting on.

John A. Macdonald in 1863.

proposals — including, in this case, the highly contentious (for PEI) issue of the number of representatives each province, and PEI especially, would have in the House of Commons.

It is not surprising, then, to find John A. and George Coles together at the party at Madame Tessier's, and returning together. Macdonald at this point was no doubt using his skills of persuasion on Coles to retain PEI's support for Confederation. It's also not surprising, then, to see John A. visiting the Coles family the next week, taking care to be there in Mercy's thoughts and writings. And it is indeed in that week when we hear more from Mercy about John A. than at any other time. It's interesting, too, how she writes of John A. Macdonald. She speaks of what he's said or done, and how it has affected her, which is not the case when she talks of Leonard Tilley.

October 26 was the last night of the conference in Quebec. On behalf of the Canadian government, Alexander Galt spent the day and evening presenting the financial resolutions, leaving out the crucial resolution, supposedly put forward at Charlottetown, for money to buy out the Island's absentee landlords. George Coles later said in the PEI legislature that "he was struck with amazement"[2] that this had been left out of the financial resolutions. It seemed that the reneging on this agreement was the final nail in the coffin for PEI's likelihood of going forward with Confederation. But not everything was certain.

There was, for example, Mercy's unspecified "conundrum," which she mentions on October 26. It leaves one wondering just what was happening here. George Coles was upset. Would Mercy have known that, and, if so, would she have known why? Was she feeling that she could help her father?

She had been meeting and conversing with Macdonald. She makes note that he brought her dessert to her, which implies she felt some level of intimacy or connection, and this is what brings up the "conundrum," after all. Did she think Macdonald liked her in *that* way, while she wasn't attracted to him romantically? It's clear she liked the attention she received, and Macdonald's attention would have given her status, but she may have been unprepared for, and unsure how to deal with, a clear move by him. Did she feel a degree of obligation to return Macdonald's feelings in order to help her father's and PEI's desires for better terms?

On his part, were Macdonald's actions out of sincere interest, or were they motivated from political expediency? The importance of the forging of relationships and allegiances during the Confederation conference in Quebec City is well known, and Macdonald was a master in creating those ties.

Politics is a game, much like courtship — a game in which the suitor comes courting, advancing and then pulling back. Perhaps the PEI delegates and Coles were still playing their chances for a better advance. It is possible that Mercy was part of that game.

Whatever the case, George Coles certainly made clear the connection between politics and romance in a speech he gave in Ottawa on November 1. In it, Coles compared Confederation to a "proposed matrimonial union," and although he conceded that "in some respects [it was] not what some of them might have wished, he hoped [it] would, taken as a whole, give satisfaction to the entire family."[3]

The PEI delegates still spoke positively in speeches, and clearly hoped things might change, but, in the end, this final action of the Canadians — the reneging on the money to buy out the landlords — cemented Prince Edward Island's opinion against Confederation.

In Mercy's extract of her diary in the *Guardian* she added this note to her entry on October 27 in Montreal:

> On arriving at the hotel I was surprised to find that I was the invalid for whom preparations had been made. Evidently Mr. Macdonald, who had *always proved a very kind friend to me* [emphasis mine], had telegraphed ahead. I found the room which had been assigned to me equipped with a large fireplace. They must have been somewhat astonished to see the invalid acting in such a sprightly way as I did.

It's hard to say whether John A. was simply courting Mercy for political expediency, or if he was truly interested in her. In terms of our political understanding, the former seems more likely, but Mercy had taken his intentions seriously to some degree.

Whatever may have been the case at the time, one is left to wonder when and how Macdonald had "always proved a very kind friend to [her]" later. He did visit Prince Edward Island, and stayed in Charlottetown after he married again (he was a widower when Mercy knew him), and perhaps Mercy and he maintained some contact. Her obituary noted that she did keep in contact with many of the men she'd met at the Confederation conferences. Nevertheless, the friendship must have been hampered by George Coles and Macdonald's later relationship, as Macdonald would write to Colonel Gray in March 1865, bidding him to say hello to those in PEI whom Macdonald knew, "always excepting Messrs. Palmer and Coles."[4]

Did Mercy truly care? Was she affected by Macdonald's attention or lack thereof? Macdonald *was* one of the most famous and charismatic men at the conference. He paid her attention, and she obviously liked receiving his attention. Mercy writes a good bit about him, and fairly openly. She feels, and one can agree with her, that Macdonald could be courting her. And there is no reason to believe that that wasn't a possibility. But it could have been strictly friendly political expediency, too. Mercy continued to write of Macdonald, and the attention he paid to her, in Ottawa, and at the end of the conference tour in Toronto.

Mercy's understanding of the situation is intriguing, because if Macdonald were serious, as she considered him to be — if he'd continued his courting, and if she hadn't been away sick — Canada's history, and perhaps Prince Edward Island's history, as well as her own, no doubt, would be different.

*Seven*

# What She Said — A Woman's Point of View

Without Mercy Coles's or Feo Monck's writings, we're left with a significantly incomplete account of the events of Confederation. Though Feo wasn't present for all of the conference goings-on, she did attend events Mercy was unable to because of her illness. Mercy's status and experience were far different from those of the upper-class Feo, but Feo is able to give us the inside look from a woman's point of view, and from that of someone not tied to the political outcomes. Her diary gives us a chance to see how Mercy and the other young women may have experienced the events.

Of the Ball at Madame Tessier's on October 19, Edward Whelan wrote in his *Union of the British Provinces*:

> All the delegates and the dignitaries of the Crown in Quebec, together with some of its best society in the private walks of life, accepted the generous invitation; and after many pleasant hours, left the ballroom with the impression that they had enjoyed one of the happiest reunions ever experienced by them.

Feo's *My Canadian Leaves*, similar to Mercy's "Extracts of a Diary" in the *Guardian*, leaves out many of her juicier, and perhaps more honest, notes. As W.L. Morton points out, her journal entries were written for the entertainment of her family, one that was "fun-loving, [and] down to earth," and a father with "literary leanings." Feo Monck's full journal entries are found in Morton's *Monck Letters and Journals, 1863–1868: Canada from Government House at Confederation*. Her apparent blitheness here about the delegates, and her disregard for Mercy's situation, have to be seen in the light of attempting to entertain her family. One could also argue that she is showing the disdain some of the British had for the uncouth Canadian colonials.

*Thursday, October 20 Quebec City**
Mr. Tessier is the "orateur" of the Upper House. I opened the ball with him opposite to Madame [Tessier] and Dick [Feo's husband, brother of, and aide, to Lord Monck]. At French parties there are no fast dances, only quadrilles and lancers; it seems so odd. The R.C. Bishop won't allow 'round' dances.... So many old people I don't think I saw and the older they were the more they danced.... Amongst others I danced with Dr. Tupper, Premier of Nova Scotia, and with Honorable Mr. Coles, leader of the Opposition in Prince Edward's Island. *I never suffered so in my life from subdued laughing as at this party. The swarms of old people dancing, with white heads!* Colonel Gray is gentlemanly. I like Dr. Tupper. *Old Coles is, I believe a retired butcher* [he was a distiller], *and oh! so vulgar I could not describe him. He is grey haired and red faced, and looks as if his legs were fastened on after the rest of his body, to support his fat....* He does steps, and gives you his hand with a bow of his head and a shake of the body. *I shall not cry when these delegates are gone; it is a bore dancing with them.* He said to me, "I'm a sort of fellow who talks away and forgets to dance." *Then he told me "has'ow my daughter is ill. What with the ship and going to see an Indian encampment, she has*

* For clarity and ease of reading, I've used italics to identify the parts that were cut out of the edited version of Feo Monck's journal published in 1891, *My Canadian Leaves*.

*diphtheria." He said "as'ow" so often and "harrd" for hard ... I bore him pretty well, till I spied Capt. Pem* [Captain Pemberton] *staring at me with a broad grin on his face, and then I broke down and laughed aloud. He never seemed to think I was laughing at him ... I had a broad smile all night long on my face by the way of being so happy, but really to hide my sufferings of restrained laughter. John A Macdonald is always drunk now,* I am sorry to say, and when someone went to his room the other night, they found him in his night shirt, with a railway rug thrown over him, practising Hamlet before a looking-glass. At the drawing-room he said to Mrs. Godley he should like to blow up Sir Robert Macdonnell* [sic] *with gunpowder; very unfortunate for this week and last; they wanted all Canadians to appear their best before the delegates.*

Of the Bachelors' Ball, Feo has much less of interest to say:

*Saturday, October 22.* The G-G opened the Ball with Madame Duval. There were 40 bachelors, not 6 as I was told. The attractions of the two rooms were supposed to be equally divided. The one room had the G-G and party, and the other the 25th string band.

Whelan offers his own take on the Bachelors' Ball in his *Union of the British Provinces*:

> The Bachelors of Quebec entertained the delegates at a ball at the Parliament Buildings on the evening of the 21st of October. His Excellency the Governor-General and his

* Christopher Moore notes in *Three Weeks in Quebec City* that this story of Macdonald may just be unfounded gossip, as nowhere else is there mention of John A. being drunk during the time in Quebec. However, just a week later, on November 1, in Ottawa, Mercy writes that he was too drunk to make a speech he was to give for the luncheon at the parliament buildings.

> ministry were present; and, indeed, all the other distinguished persons who attended the Government Ball in the same place on the 14th, participated in the hilarity happily and most successfully inaugurated by the Bachelors. The attendance was large, the display of beauty highly attractive, and the entertainment in the supper room of the best description; in short, everything combined to make the Bachelors' Ball one of the most agreeable incidents remotely connected with the convention.

Whelan's reports to his newspaper, the *Examiner,* are livelier than his later detailing of the events in his *Union of the British Provinces*. It was the Bachelors' Ball that provoked his comments on the ministers as "cunning fellows" dancing their way into the affections of the women, knowing that then, the "men will certainly become an easy conquest." These comments by Whelan certainly provide more detail and context to the otherwise "official" reports. They function as the "call," with Mercy's and Feo's diaries being the "response," showcasing their female understandings as counterpoints to official history.

It would be hard, if not impossible, to learn anything of the "other" side of the political events at Quebec and in Canada if we had to rely solely on accounts such as Edward Whelan's. It is Mercy's and Feo's voices, their points of view in telling what interests them and what they experienced, that allow for a fuller understanding of our history.

And we want Mercy back, we want her to get better, and to hear who and what is capturing her attention. Fortunately for us, and for her, Mercy and the conference-goers, finally leave the rain of Quebec City, and the first stop is the grand metropolis of Montreal.

*Eight*

# Montreal Sightseeing and the "Eighth Wonder of the World"

*Thursday, October 27 to Monday, October 31*

On Thursday, October 27, Mercy and the others finally depart Quebec City, leaving the wet and muddy "bedraggled" place behind, and Mercy is feeling better. Light begins to shine through again, and there is a joyous tone to what she writes, as she is happy again to be going to the balls, to be out, to go and see the sights. Montreal, the largest city in Canada at the time, is their first stop.

From the *Montreal Witness,* August 29, 1860, on the fireworks for the grand opening of the Victoria Bridge:

> There were many transatlantic and American visitors in the city, and their unanimous declaration was that the lighting up of Great St. James, from Victoria Square to the Place d'Armes, had never been surpassed. The sight in the harbour was magnificent; the war steamers, the Canadian Mail

steamer, and the Glasgow steamer *United Kingdom* were illuminated; while from all the decks shot up flights of rockets, and brilliant lights flashed from every port-hole. Rockets and Bengal lights were fired from St. Helen's; while from the Great Bridge the display was magnificent. Every Street added its contribution of candle light or glare of gas, so that for three hours Montreal, so to speak, heralded the arrival of the Prince of Wales [Albert Edward, oldest son of Queen Victoria] by an endless blaze of light — from horizon to zenith all was brilliant, out viewing oriental splendour and magnificence.... All the public squares were tastefully decorated with transparencies and coloured lanterns profusely interspersed among its foliage.... The dome of the City Hall was brilliantly lighted up with 3,000 jets of gas, and the windows of the large building were variegated with transparencies and Chinese lanterns.

1860 Grand Finale of Fire-Works in Honor of the Prince of Wales and the Successful Completion of the Victoria Bridge, Montreal, Canada East. Ink on newsprint — wood engraving.

The glory, the brilliance, the magnificence of Montreal! It was the largest city in Canada in 1864, with a population of ninety thousand, double the size of Toronto. Luxury hotels and ships from around the world filled her port. The biggest companies in Canada worked out of Montreal; in fact, the head offices of Canada's largest and most successful businesses were located there for the next hundred years, until the separatist conflicts of the late 1960s.

Montreal had grown by thirty-three thousand people in the ten years since 1851. Urban centres were swelling, and Montreal was growing the fastest. It was the perfect city in which to showcase the grand outlook of the 1860s: the desire to outdo nature, to highlight human potential and what people could do, flourished there. By 1860, everything was about progress, about the creation of a more perfect world. Innovation and change, the new possibilities of what the human mind and body could accomplish, were the mottos of the day. Mercy Coles and Canada were caught up in the excitement and thrall of that creation — from bridges to countries.

Bird's-eye view of Seminary gardens, Montreal, about 1870. This view was taken from the tower of Notre-Dame, and shows the city with the Victoria Bridge spanning the St. Lawrence in the background.

In Montreal, Mercy and the delegates were taken for a ride over the famous Victoria Bridge, known then as the "Eighth Wonder of the World." The Victoria Bridge, believe it or not, was, and to some extent still is, a wonder of the world. Its original piers are standing yet, and, more than 150 years later, it continues to be used for train and vehicle travel. Here in Canada, in 1860, was the longest bridge in the world. Neither the United States, with its greater number of railway lines, nor Britain, from which the engineers and designers who constructed the bridge were hired, could claim such a thing.

Before the Victoria Bridge was constructed, Montreal depended on the river for everything: trade, supplies, and transportation to the United States and the rest of Canada. There were ferries in the summer, and ice roads in the winter, to cart goods and people, but when the river wasn't usable (because it was in the process of freezing or thawing), Montreal, the growing metropolis, came to a standstill. A bridge across the St. Lawrence River seemed impossible. The river was nearly two miles across, it froze solid in winter, and it had huge ice dams when the spring came. Anything in the water would have to withstand the continued freezing and thawing, as well as the strong eleven-kilometre-per-hour current.*

Famous already for his train, the Rocket, the fastest and best locomotive in the world in the 1820s, Robert Stephenson invented an ingenious tubular bridge, one on which trains travelled through large tubes made of iron plates that were supported on piers. For the Victoria Bridge, he designed piers shaped like a ship's hull, placed at an angle, to break up the spring ice. The angle of the piers would also help move the ice downstream, and so prevent its buildup and the creation of dangerous pressure on the susceptible piers.

James Hodges, also from England, was the engineer who planned the actual building of the bridge. He wrote his own account, which is beautiful in its description of the landscape of Montreal, and detailed in the building and design of everything about it. There were cholera outbreaks, and workers suffered from snow blindness. Hodges had to deal with many disruptions, including a number involving workers striking for better pay. The work was difficult and dangerous, and in the growing economy, there were lots of other jobs to be found. Nevertheless, the miraculous Victoria Bridge was

* Today, the river isn't as wide, and the current is slower.

completed, and even completed early; the first train crossed it in December 1859. It deserved all the fanfare of its grand opening in August of 1860, with the Prince of Wales presiding. It's no wonder the people of Montreal chose the bridge as one of the main sights for the Fathers of Confederation and their families to see, and for the prince to inaugurate.

The McCord Museum in Montreal has many photographs of the construction of the bridge, thanks to William Notman, the most famous photographer in all of North America, who had his studio in Montreal. For Mercy and the delegates, having their photo taken by William Notman was a *must*. And Mercy did indeed get well enough to have her photograph taken, although she didn't think much of it. The photograph can be viewed online at the McCord Museum.

All the photographs of the people who had their pictures taken along with Mercy on October 29 are listed in Notman's ledger and are viewable online on the McCord Museum's website. This list includes Leonard Tilley who was supposed to have accompanied Mercy, "but [she] was not punctual." The photograph he sat for that day is included in chapter three.

By 1864, a person would have to sit for only six to twelve seconds in order to have his or her photograph taken. On a dreary day, he or she may have had to sit a few seconds longer. Notice that Mercy Coles isn't smiling in her photograph. Mercy's unsmiling expression was what was typical at the time. It wasn't the custom then for those having their photos taken to smile, perhaps because people weren't yet used to the idea of posing with a smile on their face, of "smiling for the camera." William Notman appears to actively discourage smiling.

Notman's advice on the subject is laid out in a pamphlet written to his clients, about 1866: "While a pleasing expression is desirable, a characteristic one is still more so, as nothing is so silly or undignified as a forced smile." He also wrote, "The one thing needful for a sitter to learn is how to forget himself. If he could be perfectly free from self-consciousness, he would secure a natural and truthful picture."[1]

The photographs of Mercy Coles (chapter one), Emma Tupper (chapter fifteen), and the others are striking in their naturalness and lack of artifice;

Christ Church Cathedral, St. Catherine Street, Montreal, about 1860. Christ Church Cathedral is an Anglican cathedral, and was built between 1857 and 1860. It has been designated as a historic site of Canada. The cathedral is unique in that it now has two floors of shopping, a mezzanine, a parking level, and the McGill metro tracks beneath it.

it's as though one can see behind the eyes, to the essence of the person. Mercy, with her head slightly tilted, looks as though you have just walked into the room and she has turned to look at you.

It's Notman's photographs of the Fathers of Confederation with which we are most familiar. He was a supreme businessman, and a huge success. By 1865, he had taken photographs of all the Fathers, and compiled them in *Portraits of British Americans*, to which he offered subscriptions. He also suggested, then got, the commission to document the making of the Victoria Bridge. He obviously loved Montreal. His photographs of his new city are an enduring testament to the grandeur and growth of the city. For someone who'd run away from Scotland in 1856 so he wouldn't be imprisoned because of a business scandal (for which his father was jailed for a short time), and who taught himself all he knew about photography, William Notman is as much an emblem of the drive in the 1860s to push the limits of human potential as is the Victoria Bridge itself.

*Thursday morning, October 27, Quebec City*
We leave for Montreal today at 4 o'clock. I had a letter from Ide this morning, they are all quite well. I was so relieved to hear of them all. Aunt Jane has arrived home all serene but has hurt her leg so can't walk very well.

*Friday morning, October 28, Montreal, St Lawrence [Hotel]*
We arrived here last night at ½ past 10. We left Quebec at 4 o'clock. I felt better as I got away. Ma would not let me talk, but I had such a nice old gentleman, Mr. Malcolm Cameron* who recited poetry for me and then entertained me with riddles.

This hotel is an immense place. We had a very nice supper when we arrived in the Hall in which we are to dance tonight. I went to

* Malcolm Cameron was the Queen's Printer in 1864. He was fifty-six years old at the time, compared to John A.'s forty-nine years, and Leonard Tilley's forty-six, so it's interesting that Mercy refers to him as an "old" man. He was pretty portly, compared to Macdonald and Tilley.

breakfast. *Mr. Tilley sat alongside of me* [emphasis mine]. He came in the night train. Dr. Tupper, Mr. Henry, and about 9 other gentlemen came. It is pouring rain so there is no going out for me today. *Mr. Crowther is here. He came to call on me this morning. He wants to hold me good for the dance I promised him at Quebec* [emphasis mine].

*Saturday morning, October 29, Montreal*

I feel quite well this morning. I went down to the Ball last night. Such a splendid affair. Mr. Crowther danced with me the first Quadrille. Sir Fenwick Williams* was here looking as well as ever. He called on us all in the afternoon. I did not stay very late at the Ball. I was engaged for every dance but I was afraid of being booked up.

Ma and I have just been to the Convent Congregation Notre Dame. Mr. McDonald (stutterer)** came and took Mamma and I. I have just come from Notman's. My photograph was not good I don't think, so I would not take it however the man said he would send me two dozen to the Island.*** Mr. Tilley was supposed

---

* Sir Fenwick Williams was sent to Canada in 1861 as commander-in-chief of the British forces in British North America. In November 1865, he was sent to be lieutenant-governor of Nova Scotia (and replace Sir Richard MacDonnell) as someone who would be pro-Confederation, of which Britain was by then in favour.

** Presumably this was Andrew Archibald Macdonald of PEI.

*** Researcher Nora Hague, who has spent many years working with the Notman Archive, and I were both delighted to discover the photograph of Mercy Coles and we were able to attach Mercy's diary notes to both Mercy's and her father's photographs. Mercy had been labelled simply as "Miss Cole," with no indication of where she was from, or anything else about her. Neither of her parents had their photos done that day, either: their identification would likely have helped to identify Mercy. The only way to determine the picture was of Mercy Coles was by looking at the Notman ledger of October 29, 1864, and finding her name, along with the other names she mentions in her diary, listed there. As the date Mercy gives is Saturday, October 29, this helped determine that Notman worked on Saturdays.

to have gone with me but I was not punctual. Andrew McDonald, Col Gray and Mrs. Pope were there before us.*

All the gentlemen are in Conference. Sir Fenwick Williams called [on] me and I saw him in the drawing room.

*Monday, October 31 [en route from Montreal to Ottawa]*

On board the *Prince of Wales* on the Ottawa River. We left Montreal this morning at seven o'clock. We came by train to Lachine then came on board this steamer. I have just seen the Rapids mentioned in the Canadian Boat Song.**

Yesterday we made the acquaintance of a Mr. Robertson at breakfast who offered us his seat at the Cathedral.*** Such a nice service. We walked around after. We saw the Church plate and the Bible presented by the Prince of Wales. We walked up to see McGill College. Such magnificent residences are in the vicinity. We went back to the Hotel in a street car. At 3 o'clock we went through the Grand Victoria Bridge. Sir R[ichard] MacDonnell and his lady went with us. We stopt in the middle and got out. We saw the rivet the Prince of Wales**** drove in, they opened the window and we looked down on a raft just passing under the bridge.

---

* Tilley, Emma Tupper and her mother, Mrs. Pope, and the others Mercy mentions all had their photos done that day at William Notman's studio.

** The rapids were at Sainte-Anne-de-Bellevue, just west of Montreal. Sainte-Anne was designated a national historic site in 1929. The "Canadian Boat Song" was written by Irish poet Thomas Moore in 1804.

*** Christ Church Cathedral now has two floors of shopping, a mezzanine, a parking level, and the McGill metro tracks beneath it. See www.montrealcathedral.ca/history.

**** The Prince of Wales, Albert Edward, reigned as King Edward VII from 1901 to 1910. At the time of his visit, he wasn't yet married; he married Princess Alexandra of Denmark in 1863.

From the 1917 *Guardian* extract:

> At the hotel we took an omnibus to go for a drive over the Victoria Bridge. One of the ladies came down to the door and said she would not go in the omnibus, and while arguing in favour of a carriage her husband stepped into the omnibus leaving her standing at the door. We passed through Griffin town, a very muddy place, and chaffed Mr. McGee on the state of his constituency. At the bridge we got out and looked at the last rivet in the construction work. It was a silver rivet which the Prince of Wales had driven when he was in Canada. They opened the windows and we looked down on a raft of timber which was just then passing under the bridge. It was a lovely day and we enjoyed the outing immensely.

These are interesting additions not in the original handwritten diary held by the LAC, and, like before, one can't really see why Mercy left these things out of her diary of the tour. Or, more to the point, how was it that her full, original diary survived as the one kept and passed on to Coles's relatives? What became of the circumscribed *Guardian* version? Very luckily for history, it is the original handwritten journal in its entirety that has been preserved.

*Nine*

# Ottawa the Unseemly

*Tuesday, November 1 to Wednesday, November 2*

Mercy and the others continue touring and sightseeing as they head farther west into the Canadas. She is happy, and full of the thrill and excitement of travel, and the balls, banquets, and courtship continue. Their first stop after Montreal is Ottawa, and the new parliament buildings, still under construction. Beyond Montreal, as they pass the rapids at Sainte-Anne-de-Bellevue, they sing the "Canadian Boat Song": "Row, brothers, row, the stream runs fast, / The Rapids are near and the daylight's past." Unlike the characters in the song, Mercy is past danger at this point, and on the road to adventure, and she can enjoy the singing as heartily as Whelan writes of the company. The weather improves, the rain stops, and they have a grand lunch in the Picture Gallery — the only finished room of the parliament buildings — and tour the locks on the Rideau Canal.

After only one day in Ottawa (it was not an impressive city by any accounts — rat-infested, with muddy roads and stinking sewers), they

Parliament buildings under construction, Ottawa 1865.

travelled to Toronto by train, with stops all along the way, and it was an exhilarating ride. The delegates' trip from Ottawa to Toronto was a big event, one we can hardly imagine today for politicians or politics. From the descriptions, you'd think they were rock stars touring across the country. Peter B. Waite eloquently wrote: "the special train … was stopped at Kingston by arrangement and at Belleville by public enthusiasm. Cheers and the waving of handkerchiefs greeted the delegates at Belleville, and bumpers* of champagne were drunk in the failing light of late afternoon on the Grand Trunk station platform."[1]

A crisp mid-fall in that part of the country is something indeed. The last of the trees are turned gold and red; yellow poplar leaves flutter in the slightest wind as the train goes past; and the travellers look out on countless

* A bumper is a glass full to the brim of an alcoholic drink and is usually drunk as a toast.

silver lakes — until Kingston, where Lake Ontario looks as big as the sea. A heady time, and a heady trip to go with it. Mercy feels as "gala" and "splendid" as her descriptions.

*November 2nd, Wednesday, [en route from Ottawa to Toronto]*
Aboard the Carslet-Prescott.* We have been travelling ever since 8 o'clock. Yesterday we had such a gala day. We went to see the Parliament Buildings in the morning, they are magnificent; such a splendid example of everything that is good. The Picture Gallery is the only room that is finished, fit to [unclear] and it was there we had the luncheon. We saw the model of the library which will be a most splendid building. It is made of plaster of Paris and is kept in a room to show what the library will be.

We went quite up to the top and saw such a nice view of Ottawa. The Chaudière Falls are very pretty and can be seen very well from there. In the halls are some marble pillars. The marble is got near Ottawa and is the prettiest I have seen. When we came out we walked round the grounds and saw the Rideau Canal which has 8 locks. We saw the place where the new barracks are to be built. We went there at 2 [more likely it was 12.00, as Whelan writes] then to luncheon. It was a grand affair. Mr. Henry, Mr. Johnston and Papa made speeches. *John A was to have made a speech but he was tight or had a palpitation of the heart and could not go on* [emphasis mine].** Mr. Galt got up and excused him very well. We went to the Ball in the evening. It was a very grand affair. I had to refuse six gentlemen

* The Ottawa and Prescott Railway was the first rail line between Ottawa and the St. Lawrence River and the towns along Lake Ontario's north shore.

** Feo Monck had written, "John A. Macdonald is always drunk now" earlier, but Christopher Moore points out that no men at the conference had suggested that Macdonald had begun drinking seriously. Nevertheless, Mercy's comment may support Feo's note, and also provides a potential reason why Macdonald was so markedly absent over the rest of the tour.

the first Quadrille. I danced it with Mr. Brydges.* His brother Mr. Dodgson had asked me to dance but I had been engaged the day before. I have kept my card which has all the names of my partners written by themselves. I had to come away with a half dozen gentlemen not danced with.

In the 1917 *Guardian* extract, Mercy leaves out her comments on John A. and adds an interesting note about her father's speech:

> On November 1st we were in Ottawa. In the picture gallery of the Parliament building we had luncheon. It was a pleasant affair, and some of the men made speeches, my father being among them. He was speaking of the allurements which they were going to hold out to the Maritime Provinces to enter Confederation. Father horrified mother and me by saying that among all the fine things we had down here [in PEI] we had the finest looking ladies, pointing to mother as a specimen. The other gentlemen said equally ridiculous things.

*Wednesday, November 2nd [Continued]*
½ past 2 — We have just dined at Kingston. Such a delicious dinner given by Mr. Brydges. Mr. Brydges has just introduced me to his uncle, such a nice person, just as nice as himself. His half-brother Mr. Dodgson is also a very nice person. Mr. Bernard has gout. He cannot put [weight] on his foot and goes hobbling around with a stick.

¼ 5 — Just arrived at Belleville. All the voluntary turned out. The Mayor presented an address. They drank the health of the mayor and started the moment after. Mr. Crowther has just given me a likeness of himself and Mr. Drinkwater will have his done again. Won a pair of gloves from Mr. Brydges. He bet that Ma was

* General manager of the Grand Trunk Railway.

lying down and I bet she wasn't. He went to see and found Mrs. [unclear] where he thought to find her.

In Edward Whelan's *The Union of the British Provinces*, the speeches at the luncheon in the parliament buildings go on for sixteen pages, and the "Dejeuner" lasts from 12:30 to 5:30! Of John A.'s "palpitations," he writes:

> The Honourable gentleman intended to have spoken at some length on the question of confederation, but illness induced by fatigue from assiduous devotion to public affairs, compelled him to curtail his observations, which the whole company deeply regretted, as no public man in Canada was considered so well qualified by talent, experience and statesmanship to speak on the question of confederation than the Honourable Attorney-General for Canada.... He [Macdonald] was applauded as if he had made the most brilliant oration ever delivered — thus manifesting the profound respect entertained for him at Ottawa.

Of Galt's excusing John A., Whelan writes: "The Hon. Mr. Galt, having expressed regret for Mr. Macdonald's illness, and having pronounced a high eulogium on the great and universally acknowledged ability of the Attorney-General West, — Mr. T.C. Clarke, rose to propose the next toast."

George Coles spoke about halfway through the speeches. As quoted in Whelan, he first talks of Confederation as a matrimonial union, and how the proposed marriage settlement, "though not what some of them might have wished, he hoped would, taken as a whole, give satisfaction to the entire family." He also speaks of how wonderful Prince Edward Island was for a summer residence, and how "plentiful the fishing off her coast."[2] There's no mention in Whelan of Coles's talk of Mercy's mother's allurements, but no doubt Coles said this.

Mercy, her family, and the delegates travelled from Quebec through to Toronto by rail in special cars provided for them by Charles Brydges, general manager of the Grand Trunk Railway. The railways in Canada then, especially the Grand Trunk and the Great Western, were vying for business, wanting to be the one chosen for the intercolonial railway, which would extend across the Maritimes and west, beyond the borders of western Ontario. It was a big business, and required just as much deal making and relationship building as Confederation. It was a business of promises, of compromises, and of patronage — the whole Pacific Scandal was yet to come — and Charles Brydges, who had been the manager of the Great Western just two years earlier, was doing his utmost to make the Grand Trunk the chosen line. The railway men knew, too, that paying attention to the women was an important part of the negotiations. The Mr. Livesay of whom Mercy wrote, who paid her so much attention, was also a railway man.

According to the *Canadian Encyclopedia*, by Confederation, in 1867, "The GTR was the world's largest railway system, with 2,055 km of track. By the late 1880s [by which time the GTR and the Great Western Railway had merged] it had grown to more than 700 locomotives, 578 cars, 60 post-office cars, 131 baggage cars, 18,000 freight cars, and 49 snow plows. The GTR ran unbroken from the Great Lakes at Sarnia, to the Atlantic coast Portland, Maine."

As in any battle for control, there were intense animosities, blame, and recrimination. The railways were owned by companies in Britain, and managed by men sent to Canada to oversee the building and running of the lines. The need for expansion, and speedy expansion at that, was expensive. This created a lot of room for dissatisfaction in the quality, cost, and management of the lines.

Brydges was thirty-seven years old in 1864, and had immigrated to Canada in 1852, when he became managing director of the Great Western Railway (a rival of the Grand Trunk at the time). Charles Brydges has been described variously as someone who was too ambitious, too aggressive, and in part responsible for the eventual bankruptcy of the Grand Trunk, as well as making the GTR much more efficient and caring toward its workers. He established schools, libraries (called reading rooms), and pensions for injured and older workers. He felt he had a responsibility to contribute to the betterment of the world he lived in, and proved that by his actions. Brydges was married, with seven young children, in 1864, so he wasn't "courting" Mercy in that sense, but it's clear that he and Mercy enjoyed each other's company. The building of positive relationships could only help his cause.

*Ten*

# Sightseeing in Toronto, 1864 Style

*Thursday, November 3*

Mercy and the delegates arrived in Toronto at 10 o'clock at night, in style. They were accompanied to the Queen's Hotel by a torchlight procession of five thousand people! There were brass bands and fireworks. The obviously impressed — maybe even star-struck — Nova Scotian delegate Johnathan McCully said the next day at the banquet given for the delegates, "We have been received with a continued ovation; it has been one carnival, from the beginning till now."[1]

In Toronto, the whole group was taken on a whirlwind sightseeing tour. They went to Osgoode Hall, Upper Canada College, the Normal School (containing all of Egerton Ryerson's eclectic collections of miniature implements and curiosities), and the music hall in the Mechanics' Institute, which was the forerunner of the Toronto Public Library. The Normal School was the future Ontario Institute for Studies in Education, as well as the future Royal Ontario Museum.

Osgoode Hall, Toronto, about 1860.

*Toronto, Queen's Hotel, Thursday November 3rd*

We arrived at Mr. Cockburn's* last night at 8 o'clock. Such a beautiful place, he gave us a magnificent supper the only pity was we had such a short time to stay. They had illuminations and all sorts of grandeur. We arrived here at 10 o'clock. Such a grand affair torch light procession. 5,000 people were in front of the hotel. Dr. Tupper, Mr. Tilley and Mr. Brown made speeches from a gallery just beneath my bedroom window.

We have just had breakfast and are now off sightseeing.

8 o'clock I am just going to dress for the Ball.

* James Cockburn, solicitor general for Canada West.

We started off this morning to visit the Public Institutions, first we went to the Public School [Upper Canada College]. All the elder boys formed a guard of honour from the gate to the entrance by the Professors. We went to the schoolroom and the head master read an address to which Col Gray PEI replied. The boys received a holiday and we started for the Lawyer's Hall [Osgoode Hall], a splendid building, the centre hall is right up to the roof stained glass in the dome. The floor is mosaic.* They showed us the library and the Judges rooms. We drove from there to the University. It is a splendid building, nearly as handsome as the Ottawa Departmental Building. There all the students wore caps and gowns. The doctor made a very nice speech to us to which Dr. Tupper replied.** We then visited the Museum in which is a very fine collection of birds and small animals. The Butterflies were beautiful.*** We had to hasten away for time was short. The students formed a line and cheered us as we drove down the avenue. From there we went to the normal school which is certainly the most varied institution I ever saw. It combines a Picture Gallery, a statutory Gallery, all kinds of miniature implements and nearly everything one can think of that is curious. The little boys and girls sang when we went to their school rooms. I saw a boy who looked so much like Russell [Mercy's young brother]. We had to hurry back to the Hotel for the gentlemen had to go to the Music Hall**** to luncheon. Ma and I had a carriage and went for a drive and to do some shopping. We went to the luncheon for about an hour, heard Mr. Palmer, Carter, a Red River

---

* You can still see the stained-glass dome and the mosaic floor in Osgoode Hall. They are in the Benchers' Wing, which is the oldest part of the building.

** Whelan notes this was in Convocation Hall. The current Convocation Hall at the University of Toronto was built in 1907.

*** According to Whelan, they also saw the library and the observatory.

**** The music hall was in the Mechanics' Institute, at the northeast corner of Church and Adelaide — which also housed Toronto's Free Library, which became the Toronto Public Library.

> man Louis Riel* and part of a speech from Mr. Brown. Mr. Bernard was waiting in the parlour for us when we came home and took us down to dinner. He has been laid up with the gout for three days. *He looks awful. I tease him about it, it is a great shame but I can't help it* [emphasis mine].**

Whelan's reports of the same visits provide more context. Two hundred some students at Upper Canada College "were ranged on either side [of the carriageway], all having Enfield rifles, which they carried at the 'present'.... " Whelan said of the Normal School, "[though] not so attractive in architectural construction as the University, the interior arrangements and objects of interest were of a more diversified character, and attracted much longer attention."

The Normal School, founded by Egerton Ryerson, was for the training of teachers. It eventually became the Toronto College of Teachers, which later became OISE, the Ontario Institute for Studies in Education. Its history is really the history of education and art in Ontario. Mercy's comment calling it "the most varied institution" puts it mildly. The pictures, statues, miniatures, and all the other odd things Mercy writes of were collected by Ryerson himself on trips to Europe in the 1850s. This collection eventually led to the creation of the Royal Ontario Museum; the Ontario School of Art, which became the Ontario College of Art and Design; and the Ontario Agricultural College, which then became part of the University of Guelph. The Normal School building itself is no longer in existence, but part if its facade forms the Ryerson University arch, at the entrance to the athletics building.

Now, whether Louis Riel was actually at the talks in Toronto is a matter of speculation. Riel had only just turned twenty, and was supposed to be in school at the seminary in Montreal, but he was often absent. His father had died in January of 1864, and Riel was upset, and not doing well. None

* Whelan says this was James Ross; more on this later.

** Hewitt Bernard's notes on the conference meetings end on Tuesday, October 25. Perhaps he was already sick. His gout was likely rheumatoid arthritis.

of Louis Riel's papers from this time survive. But there is no reason Mercy Coles would know of Riel in 1864 if she hadn't heard his name. It's clear from her handwritten diary that she wrote his name after the original diary entry, as it is written above "a Red River man." But just when after the fact did she write it? In 1869, Emma Tupper went with her husband, Donald Cameron (William McDougall's right-hand man in setting up the Boundary Commission, which set the stage for the Red River Rebellion), to Pembina, Manitoba, and there they had a run-in with Riel. Maybe Mercy knew of this, and added the name Riel then, for certainly by 1869, Riel was widely known. There's no way of knowing if Mercy added Riel's name later on the same day that she wrote the diary entry, or later that week. If this were the case it would seem more likely that Riel was in Toronto. In comparison, Mercy writes of Abraham Lincoln's re-election while she and her family travel through the States, and although he was assassinated only five months later, she didn't add anything to her diary about that.

It's clear from the speech that Whelan quotes in his *Union of the British Provinces* that James Ross was at this Toronto event. Ross was a former editor of the *Nor'Wester* in Red River, and was reading law in Toronto at the time. In his speech at the banquet Ross says he is the only representative from Red River there. Louis Riel, however, was not against the idea of Confederation in 1864, and he knew and supported George-Étienne Cartier; it thus remains a bit of an unsolved mystery whether Riel may also have been in Toronto. It's unlikely, but possible.

*Eleven*

# Niagara Falls

*Friday, November 4*

After Toronto, the Maritimers, with dignitaries from Hamilton, St. Catharines, and Welland, go on to Niagara Falls for the grand finale of the official tour of the Canadas. As everything has only just begun for her a week earlier, Mercy is loath to have it all stop. She has been recording all the events and places, what's been done and said, and she wants to go on filling and filling her dance card.

Mercy writes of Macdonald one last time, at the end of their tour in Toronto. He'd chosen to ride in the carriage with her and her mother on the trip from Cobourg to Toronto, on Wednesday, November 2. There would have been a number of carriages, and Macdonald chose to travel with Mercy's group. This was a day after he had "a palpitation" in Ottawa and could not give his speech. Was this decision to ride with her another indication of possible courting? Interestingly, even though Macdonald did go to Toronto, he gave no speeches there. He didn't go on any of the sightseeing events Mercy and Whelan write of, and he didn't attend the big luncheon at the music hall. He indeed may have been drunk in Ottawa, as Mercy speculated. Macdonald often started on a drinking binge, not when something was finished, but as he got increasingly tired. Certainly he'd been working hard at the conference talks for the sixteen days in Quebec City, and the four weeks previous preparing the way for the talks. He may well have been disappearing into drink, as he did not return to his office until over a week later.

*Friday, November 4th, Great Western Railway*
*[en route from Toronto to Niagara Falls]*
11 o'clock we started from Toronto this morning at 10 o'clock. We expect to get to Kingston [Hamilton] in 2 hours. We had a glorious Ball last night. I danced every dance and had several engaged when I came away. Mr. Bernard had told one of the stewards about me. He got Mr. Brydges to introduce him and then he got me partners for every dance, the ladies were dressed to death and some of them were very pretty. The music was not as good as I expected, the 16th Regiment. We did not get home until nearly three o'clock. I am so sorry we part from the party today at Niagara Falls. Most of them go back to Toronto. We go to Ohio. I should like to have gone home with the party but that is impossible. *I have not seen John A. since he came up in the carriage with us at Cobourg. He did not appear at all yesterday. Mr. Bernard was at the station this morning to say good bye. I told him to say everything kind for me to John A* [emphasis mine].

By the 1917 *Guardian* extract, Mercy is editing what she says about the people and events of the conference and tour. Mercy's detailed note and reference to John A. in her diary becomes:

> I did not see Mr. J.A. Macdonald, but Mr. Bernard said he had asked him to say good-bye.

The diary continues:

*Buffalo, 8 o'clock, Friday, November 4*
We have just arrived here from Niagara. We got to Niagara at 2 o'clock. There was a very nice luncheon given by Mr. Swinyard, the manager of the Great Western Railway. Directly after lunch we got into carriages and drove to the falls. I can't it is quite impossible to describe them. They far exceeded anything I expected to see. I saw them from all points. Mr. Swinyard took me down under the falling water on Table Rock. Such fun as we had getting up and down the stairs. He painted my name on the inside of the place where we went down. It was raining the whole time but we did not mind. The water in the middle of the Great Horse Shoe was a splendid aqua marine color — and looked as if it was beautifully fluted. After we saw everything there was to be seen we drove to Mr. Streets,* a gentleman who has the most beautiful grounds I ever saw — beautiful suspension bridges, little platforms right on the very edge of the rapids, it was such fun the boards were so slippery with the rain it was almost impossible to stand. Ma and Pa both fell, a gentleman went to help them, his heels slipped up and down he came. *Mr. Swinyard took very good care of me. He is such a very nice man. I took quite a fancy to him* [emphasis mine]. After we had seen all that was to be seen we drove back to the station. There we had to say goodbye to all the party and take the train for here. The Tuppers are gone to New York, Col Grey [*sic*] is going to stay a few days at Niagara, all the rest have gone back to Toronto, perhaps we shall go back that way. We remain here at this Hotel Mansion until 12 o'clock. We then take the cars for Cleveland.

Mercy clearly still hoped she and her parents might yet return to Toronto, where perhaps there would be social events, with the possibility of more opportunities for courtship. Many of the other Maritimers, along with most of the single young women and the widowed Mrs. Alexander, were

* Thomas Clark Street, a lawyer and businessman who was the first MP for Welland after Confederation.

returning the way they had come — back to Toronto, then Montreal and Quebec, and on to the east coast. Leonard Tilley; Thomas Haviland and his sister, Mrs. Mary Alice Alexander; William Steeves and his two daughters; Adams Archibald and his daughter Joanna; Charles Fisher and his daughter Jane; and Charlotte Gray, and her father, Colonel Gray of New Brunswick, were returning via Toronto. Mercy misses their company, and whatever last chances there might be for her.

George Brown's *Globe* wrote on Saturday, November 5, in "Excursion of the Delegates to Niagara Falls," that Swinyard had lined up "a special train, consisting of the official car of the company and three splendid new first-class cars. The engine was tastefully decorated with evergreens and flags.…" Not a "glorious" ball, but there were still good times to be had.

Mercy writes she "took quite a fancy to" Thomas Swinyard, the general manager of the Great Western Railway. Swinyard was thirty-one years old and married with children in 1864. In 1873, when PEI joined Confederation, he was appointed by the federal government to assess the PEI railway. We don't know whether Mercy had any contact with him then, but by her 1917 recollections, all Thomas Swinyard gets is, "At Buffalo we saw the falls: a Mr. Swinyard accompanied us."

Street's gardens, to which Mercy refers, are still in Niagara Falls, with their walkways through the woods, little wooden bridges, and views of the top of the falls. There are no more platforms or suspension bridges; nevertheless, the view of the falls and rapids above them is impressive. Thomas Street became the first member of Parliament for Welland in 1867. A portion of Street's house is part of the mansion that mining multi-millionaire Sir Harry Oakes built in the 1920s, and the grounds are part of the Niagara Parks Commission. The "gardens" are now the Dufferin Islands. Oak Hall is the administration office for the Niagara Parks Commission. The ground floor of the house is open to the public. There is a teak table on which the Boxer Rebellion Treaty (bringing peace to unrest in China) was signed in 1901, as well as the twelve chairs used at a luncheon in 1919 to honour the Prince of Wales (later King Edward VIII, who abdicated to marry Wallis Simpson in 1937). There are lots of paintings and pictures of Niagara Falls and the surrounding area done by leading artists in the 1800s and 1900s. But there is not a word on the fact that the Fathers of Confederation visited in November

1864. Whelan has a small note on it, and the *Globe* of November 5 mentions it. Mercy's diary is the only one to give this detailed account of the day and of the garden. Thomas Street's garden was well-known as a tourist attraction in 1864, and Feo Monck also writes of visiting it in her journal when she and a party were visiting Niagara Falls for a week, from Thursday, October 6, to Wednesday, October 12, 1864.

> We [Feo; her husband, Dick; and Lord Lyons, the British ambassador to Washington] all sallied out to see the Island [Goat Island, by the American falls], where the rapids rush past you in the walk, and make you giddy under shaky bridges. It is beautiful and peculiar.... I think Mr. Street had not shown good taste in putting fantastic seats about near the curious rapids and among the wonderful underwood and trees at the waters' edge: it looks too like a tea garden business.[1]

Feo was also very impressed by Niagara Falls:

> I almost felt as if I must say, in the Litany, "Oh! Thou who madest Niagara, have mercy upon us." I say this in all reverence. It was better than any sermon, seeing what we saw today. The falls are magnificent, when you are close to them, and the rapids really too wonderful. The little bits of red colouring made everything look twice as beautiful.

Later she adds,

> We had another look at the falls from the Canadian side; they are more and more beautiful and grand every time you look at them. The water in parts of them is of the deepest green!

Mercy's joie de vivre, humour, and sense of adventure come through in her account of Niagara. She doesn't mind the rain. They go merrily tripping across bridges and platforms over the rapids, slipping on the wet stone under Table Rock. She's joyous and happy to be out and participating in everything, noting all the interesting things to see, with little time for reflection. She's twenty-six, with the thrill of everything heightened after her illness.

Nevertheless, as much as Mercy wants to continue with the group, she and her parents leave Niagara Falls, and go on alone.

*Twelve*

# Family and Travel

*Saturday, November 5 to Thursday, November 10*

The end of the tour has come for the delegates, the party is over, and they are returning home, separately or in small groups, to their former lives. The politicians will now have to work for (or against) Confederation, both with their legislatures and the people of their provinces. Leonard Tilley will lose dramatically at the polls in 1865, and this will cause a whole rethinking of the Confederation timeline. Macdonald — all of them — had hoped for a resolution, a concrete step toward Confederation in 1865, but that wasn't to be. Macdonald and the others blamed Tilley for calling an election in New Brunswick on the issue, instead of just fighting it out in the legislature. But Tilley had lost the support of his followers in the legislature, and going to the electorate was the only choice he figured he had. He lost, and his government fell. Historian Christopher Moore examined Tilley's options and determined, like Tilley, that there was nothing else he could do. Maybe Macdonald, with hindsight, would agree with Tilley. At any rate, 1865 was an impossibility. The

Fathers (but not any of the Prince Edward Island delegates) eventually went to London in the late fall of 1866 to present the British North America Act to the British Parliament for approval. The delegates to the London Conference stayed through the winter, and the motion was finally passed on March 12, 1867, with Queen Victoria giving her royal assent on March 29. She also declared the country's official "birth date" would be July 1, 1867.

The British colonial secretary responsible for helping the Canadian delegation prepare and present its Confederation proposals to the British House of Commons was Henry Howard Molyneux Herbert, 4th Earl of Carnarvon. Lord Carnarvon hosted Macdonald at his country estate, Highclere Castle, for a weekend in December 1866. Highclere Castle is the setting for the popular television show *Downton Abbey*, with Lord Grantham as a fictional earl. High times were to be had back in Lord Carnarvon's time, too; it was after that weekend that Macdonald accidentally set his bedclothes and bed on fire at his hotel in London. (He was fine, though he did have some third-degree burns.)

The Coles family travelled through the United States to Warren, and to Bloomfield, Ohio, to visit Mercy's mother's relatives. The second week, on their way back home, they toured Boston and New York City, seeing Barnum's Circus and a show on Broadway. Nevertheless, Mercy was sad to part with the group. We also see why she didn't write more about Leonard Tilley during the last weeks of the conference: another woman had taken, even demanded, his attention.

This first week is full of the family visit at Clover Hill Farm in Bloomfield. Mercy's mother's older brother, William Haine, emigrated from England to Bloomfield, Ohio, in 1835, after staying in Prince Edward Island for a time. The Haines were from Somerset, England, as were George Coles's parents. Many of the families mentioned by Mercy on this visit also emigrated from Somerset (Dunkerton, Haine, Hawkins, and Symes), and thus a lot of them were related to each other. Many married their first cousins, too. Mercy's uncle, William Haine, married his first cousin, Mary Haine, so the interconnections were extensive, to say the least. A family history book by an American relative, *A Journey from Somerset, England to Ohio: For the Hawkins and Haine Family, 1700–2000*,* reports that Mercy's mother and father

* Mercy's uncle, William, was author Sue Hawkins Bell's great-great-grandfather (26).

visited Clover Hill Farm in 1848. George Coles travelled to Massachusetts and Ohio in the Fall of 1848, and it was his visits there that led to the ideas for his Free Education Act, passed in PEI in 1852. Unfortunately for Mercy's story, there is nothing in Bell's book about their visit in 1864.

There are a whole lot of cousins, aunts, and uncles mentioned in Mercy's diary, along with simple notes on family visits, gossip, and sing-alongs — a typical family reunion. What's interesting is the very different lives the American relatives are leading from the Canadian Coleses, although there is very little reference by either Mercy, or the family, to those different circumstances. The Civil War was in full swing. Brothers, husbands and beaus were off fighting, being captured, killed — all the usual things that happen in war. Mercy's cousin, Frances, kept a diary until her marriage in 1863. She wrote of her concern over her two brothers, William and George, who had enlisted in 1862, and of George's capture. By the fall of 1864, Mercy says only that they were away, and were clerks in the war office. After the Sunday sermon on August 3, 1862, Frances Haine wrote:

> "If it be possible, live peaceable with all men...." Yet there are times when it is right to take up arms. It is not right for us to let the South tyrannize over us and make slaves of us. We should feel it a privilege to defend our government which is the BEST in the world. If anything is worth fighting for, surely this is. He [the pastor] then tried to arouse the young men to a sense of duty. The call is for 600,000. It does seem hard to see our young men going to die and suffer for our country. I want our country to be saved but still I dislike for any of my friends to go — which shows how selfish I am. But I do hope this is the last call.

The sermon must have moved her brothers, William and George, as they left, along with sixteen other men from Bloomfield, for the camp in Warren on August 11. William had just decided to marry, and the ceremony was held that same evening, August 11, in Warren, before he left for the war. Frances and a group of friends joined with her brothers in Warren to celebrate the wedding. She wrote, "It did not seem like much of a wedding to me. It was so sad to think that William was going to War the next morning. There was a great war meeting that evening and the drums were beating and the cannons were firing at the time they were married. The horrors of war took away all the pleasures of the occasion...."

On October 21, they hear one of the local boys has been killed, William has been wounded, and another local boy who'd been wounded had died. A week later, on October 26, they have a letter from George that says he's been sick with lung fever. As well, "He gives a hard account of the rebels that are stealing, and destroying everything they can."

On December 31, 1862, Frances wrote, "[The year] brought many sorrows to our community.... I am thankful both my brothers have been spared when so many have been cut down."

Mercy's relatives had been touched significantly by the ongoing war, and yet, there was nothing in Mercy's diary to suggest either she, or her relatives, were concerned. Mercy seems unaware of the implications the war held for people's lives. Was she ignorant? Naive and innocent? Certainly, she was smarter than that. She sang the "Bonnie Blue Flag"* at her Uncle William's — presumably a Union version — and its lyrics leave no doubt about the aim and scope of the war.

Here are two typical Union stanzas:

We trusted you as brothers,
Until you drew the sword,
With impious hands at Sumter
You cut the silver cord.
So now you hear the bugles,
We come the sons of Mars,
To rally round the brave old flag
That bears the stripes and stars.

---

* The original "Bonnie Blue Flag" was a Confederate song written in 1861. Union versions developed in response. All the songs were full of fighting to the death and for justice and right.

Chorus: Hurrah, Hurrah,
For equal rights hurrah,
Hurrah for the good old flag
That bears the stripes and stars.
We do not want your cotton,
We do not want your slaves,
But rather than divide the land,
We'll fill your Southern graves.
With Lincoln for our chieftain,
We wear our country's stars,
And rally round the brave old flag
That bears the stripes and stars.

And two stanzas of the Confederate version:

We are a band of brothers and native to the soil
Fighting for our Liberty, with treasure, blood and toil
And when our rights were threatened, the cry rose near
and far
Hurrah for the Bonnie Blue Flag that bears a single star!
Chorus: Hurrah! Hurrah!
For Southern rights, hurrah!
Hurrah for the Bonnie Blue Flag that bears a single star.
As long as the Union was faithful to her trust
Like friends and like brethren, kind were we, and just
But now, when Northern treachery attempts our rights
to mar
We hoist on high the Bonnie Blue Flag that bears a single star.

Mercy wrote that her cousin, Frances's brother, George Haine, a clerk in the war department, was supposed to come see them, but didn't. It's not clear where he was at that time in November 1864, but this was the time when the 105th Ohio Voluntary, in which he'd enlisted, was moving from Chattanooga, TN, to support General Sherman in the destruction of Atlanta and the big "March to the Sea." She wrote that another cousin,

Bertie Symes, had been "two months at Chattanooga." Life overall for her relatives was definitely not the simple, happy time they showed Mercy and her parents, and one surmises the Coles family would be aware of that difference.

This is an excerpt of a letter from a soldier, Charles Caley, of the 105th, from November 12 to 16, to his wife, Juliaette Carpenter Caley:

> Near Savannah Dec 18th 64
> My Dear Wife
> As I came inn [*sic*] from picket yesterday I found Some leters [*sic*] waiting inn Camp for me three from you and one from Brother John also the Sage you sent and also the paper you Sent. you wished me to give you an account of our march and campaign So I wil [*sic*] begin to day Nov. 12th we Commenced our long and tiresom [*sic*] march we broke camp at Kingston about 8 o.clock every thing being cleaned out when about two milds [*sic*] out we could See the black Smoak [*sic*] looming up like a cloud and als [*sic*] the red flame which reached to the tops of the highest trees it was a grand Sight for us Soldiers we marched all day hard and camped that night on the Altona mountains it was a very cold raw windy night I was on camp guard and it was all I could do to keep from freezing
>
> Nov 13th we got up early and got our breakfast and was ready to march at day light we went through the pass and marched out from altona about three milds haldet [*sic*] and began taring [*sic*] up the rail road Taring up our own line of Communication and as you may Say Cutting off our own Supplyes [*sic*] of life in the enamys [*sic*] Country and entirely cut off from every Communication but yet we went on piled up the ties and piled the rails on the top and burnt them.... [W]e burn all litel [*sic*] towns as [we] passed through.
>
> Nov 14th we got up and ready to march at day light marched through Marietta that pretty litel town was all

> inn flames and the crashing of falling buildings flame and Smoke made it a horible [*sic*] Sight....
>
> Nov. 15th got into Atlanta about noon found a part of the town burnt and the fire was runing [*sic*] like a huricane [*sic*].... Atlanta was burnt to ashes before day light of the 16th.

These descriptions by Caley contrast so sharply with Mercy's talk of singing the "Bonnie Blue Flag" as if it were a lark — something fun to sing and with which to regale each other — that it's difficult to put the two images together. The blitheness of Mercy's and her relative's portrayals of life versus the reality of the war is hard to understand. Mercy's uncle would, at the very least, have known how things were, as the newspapers were printing the war activity within a few days of events. Frances's earlier diary entries make it clear she knew, to some extent, how bad things were for the soldiers. Nevertheless, we get a glimpse here into the massive gap between life as it was being experienced and how it was being portrayed, at least to visitors, as well as into the chasm between the lives of the soldiers and those at home.

Mercy hedges, in her writing, about what she wants to discuss, and doesn't tell us directly what we want to know. She gives details of events — whether of the conference, the tour, or the family visit — which, at times, given what we know now, make her appear blithe, naive, or even ignorant. We know this isn't the case, from her astute observations and adroit detailing of people and their behaviour. She is painting a picture of life, and of herself, as carefree, light, and airy. She is creating the identity she wishes to have, writing her own self-image.

Feo Monck's diaries are similar in ways. She, too, was creating a portrait of herself in a new place, mocking her own (and others') weaknesses, being self-effacing when she clearly was not insignificant or timid at all. The difference between the two journals and writers lies in the direct way in which Feo details the effect people and events have on her, and the others in her circle. But Feo's diaries were written for an audience, and were meant to entertain and inform people at home about life in Canada. Mercy's style of writing is for a personal diary, one to remind the writer herself of places and the time. But one wishes Mercy would give up her breezy portrayal of herself and the world, and tell us, as Feo does, more about the world of which she is part.

As noted earlier, Margaret Gray, daughter of Colonel Gray of PEI, also kept diaries. Evelyn MacLeod, in *One Woman's Charlottetown: Diaries of Margaret Gray Lord, 1863, 1876, 1890,* annotates three of Gray's diaries. MacLeod notes: "The entries in these diaries [1863, 1876, 1890] are simple and spare, and unfortunately they do not reveal much of their writer's personality. Only rarely does Margaret write about her concerns, opinions, or ambitions...."[1] Even a much-anticipated trip to England, when she was eighteen years old, has Margaret writing in her "simple and spare" fashion. Her style of reportage, when just listing the essential details of an event, is similar to Mercy Coles's at times. Overall, however, in the 1863 Gray diary, there appears to be no attempt to create a self-image, or any attempt to devise a picture of life, breezy or otherwise. By comparison, Mercy is quite free in her writing, talking of teasing, and wanting attention, and who was drunk when. Her journal, even with its limitations, is a hotbed of commentary, thoughts, and feeling. She appears as a young woman wanting to break free of the stereotypes placed on women at the time, at least in terms of her discursive identity.

> *Saturday, November 5th,*
> *[en route from Niagara Falls to Cleveland, Ohio]*
> On board the cars for Cleveland. We did not go on last night. The landlord at the Hotel told Pa we could just as well go on this morning so we remained at the Hotel all night and started at 6 this morning. We expect to get to Uncles before dark. It is a splendid day. The sun is rising splendidly. *I feel so lonesome this morning without the familiar group. I wonder if they are thinking of me this morning. Mr. Tilley will have enough to do to take care of Mrs. Alexander* [emphasis mine].

Mercy obviously hopes Leonard Tilley is thinking about her, wants him to be thinking of her, even if he is busy with the "care" of Mrs. Alexander.

Clearly, Mrs. Alexander has been dominating and demanding Tilley's attention, and Mercy has missed his company and his "taking care" of her as he did at the very first event, where "Mr. Tilley took charge of me and walked about with me the whole evening." One doesn't have to do much reading between the lines to see there was a lot of manoeuvring for the men's attention, from the Mr. Carver the Steeves sisters were "monopolizing," to Mrs. Alexander needing "care."

> 9 o'clock, here we are stopt in the road. Something is the matter with the engine. We have been here nearly a half an hour. Such a thing did not happen before since we left home. The Grand Trunk is the line. I have not much faith in Yankee Railways. They have sent back to the Station to get another engine. We are going backwards now. I must say it is not very lively to be brought to a full stop in this way. Another engine has come up and we are off again. We intended to stop at Painesville but a man said it would be nearer to go to Cleveland. We arrived at Cleveland at 3 and are now in the train for Warren. It is a splendid day, such a difference from the Canadian weather. Cleveland is a nice city, a great many more factories and some very nice shops. The streets are very wide.

> *Sunday Morning, November 6, Warren, Ohio*
> Warren We arrived here last night at 8 o'clock, it was too late to go on to Bloomfield so we remained here all night. We start for Bloomfield this morning for Mr. Dunkerton's which is 15 miles [to the north]. It is a beautiful morning.

> *Monday, November 7, 1864, Bloomfield, Ohio*
> We arrived here at Uncle Dick's [Dunkerton] yesterday at noon, it was a long drive and indeed I was very glad when the driver

announced we had arrived. Aunt Elizabeth [Haine] is quite an old woman. I think I should have known her by her photograph. Uncle Dick is an original, he reminds me very much of Gr[and]papa. He was so delighted to see mamma, so was Aunt. They had almost given us up. They have 4 children [at home]. 2 boys, 2 girls. Sarah is quite a housekeeper. Jane is very much like mamma only not so rosy. The boys are half grown. In the afternoon Uncle William arrived. I was not a bit disappointed in him, he is just as I [unclear] he was, a large, stout healthy looking man, very handsome. His wife is a very nice woman. We all go there to dine and stay all night to night. They ate crackers and cheese this morning. No servants, here they all do their own work. I am not surprised Bertie found it so different at our house where he had a half a dozen to work on him. I am so sorry he isn't here, he has been away 2 months at Chattanooga. His sister Mary was married a fortnight ago yesterday. Aunt has promised to send and let his other sister know we are here so she may come to see us.

*Tuesday, November 8, 1864, Bloomfield, Ohio*

We drove to Uncle William's yesterday and arrived just in time for dinner. They have such a nice house. After dinner, Lottie and Ellen arrived from Farmington. Lottie is such a nice girl so much like Loo.* They sang a nice melo[ioe / melody?] and in the evening we had such nice singing. Frances Haine now Mrs. Hawkins,

* Loo is Mercy's sister Louisa, born 1844. Lottie (Charlotte) and Ellen are Mercy's cousins, the daughters of William and Mary Haine. Charlotte was nineteen years old, and Ellen fifteen. (Ellen died of tuberculosis just two years later, in 1866.) Frances Haine Hawkins, twenty-three years old, was an older sister of Charlotte and Ellen's. She married Thomas Goddard Hawkins in 1863 and they were living with his parents at Farmington. Both Frances and her mother, Mary Haine, kept diaries, but there are none preserved of the Coles family's visit in 1864. (Frances stopped writing diaries once she married in 1863, but continued again many years later.)

William Haine's wife and her baby and another Mrs. Hawkins and her husband, Sarah Symes, and Bertie's sister Mrs. Cook* and her children. Aunt Dunkerton's daughter was there. Bertie's beau Annie Creighton was there and her brother. We were such a large party. Uncle William is the dearest old man I ever met. Lottie and I left together and didn't we chat.

Uncle took us to his mill, he has a mill where he grinds corn and wheat. Ma and I were weighed. Ma 220. Mine 138. Aunt Elizabeth 194. Aunt Sarah [is] as stout as Ma but she does not weigh as much. *The Presidential Election came off today. Uncle William and Pa went to the Poll. I think they were pretty much all the same way, very few seats for Mr. [George B.] McClellan* [emphasis mine].**

We left Uncle Williams about 4 o'clock. He was very sorry to part with me and I was very sorry to leave. He coaxed me very much to stay all winter but Pa and Ma would not hear of it. Uncle and Aunt are coming down tomorrow morning to go with us to Warren. They are dear good people. It rained all the morning and I cd not go out. I wanted to go to see Frances and Annie Creighton. Aunt Mary's [Haine] youngest boy is Charlie, just the size and age of our Charlie [born in 1859]. Clara is like Dina [Mercy's sister Georgianna], [Ursula?] is like her father. There is only another boy at home, Johnny, not quite so big as Willie Dunkerton. Brothers George and William Haine are clerks in the War Department. George was expected today but he did not come.

George Dunkerton is a very fine young man. He goes to school at Farmington. He will make a very fine young man.

Uncle Dick Dunkerton is the jolliest old card I ever met. He said when we wanted to go early to Uncle William's yesterday "I don't want to go there before dinner is ready. I hate having to [unclear] waiting for my meals". He had several bad pains after

---

* Mary Dunkerton, who'd married Thomas Cook.

** So much for the election! Abraham Lincoln was re-elected, winning 212 of the 233 Electoral College votes. Lincoln's success in this election was attributed, in part, to General Sherman's taking of Atlanta for the Union.

dinner and had to get a glass of punch. Indeed, since we have been in Bloomfield there is nothing but eating and drinking. We stay here at Aunt Elizabeth's and leave from Warren tomorrow afternoon.

*November 9th, Wednesday night, Warren, Ohio*
We arrived here at 6 o'clock. They were very loath to part with us and it is a pity for we need not have left until tomorrow morning for there is a special train leaves at 12 o'clock. Pa thinks to go by the 9 o'clock train. Uncle William, Aunt Mary and George Dunkerton are here with us. William Haine arrived last night. He came down to Uncle Richard's this morning with his wife and [unclear]. He looks very pale and very much as he looks in his likeness. I saw the whole connections but George Haine and Bertie Symes. [Unclear] Symes came to see us this morning. He is not the least like Bertie but seems a very nice person. Aunt Mary brought me a little bottle of honey for my throat. Last night I had a dose of [unclear]. Ma rubbed my throat outside with it and went off to bed. It is better today. They made me sing "Bonnie Blue Flag's" lyric at Uncle William's and that hurt my throat. Last night all the girls came down from Uncle William's and we had such a jolly time. Uncle William wanted me to stay with him until this morning but Papa thought I had better go with he and Ma. Uncle just wanted me to go out with him and after I was ready and all, Pa said it was too damp and I had to take off my things again.

Mercy's uncle, William, wished her to stay the winter, stay overnight, go for a walk.... But each time, her parents said no. Mercy never says whether she wanted to or not. She does the things requested of her — gets ready for a walk, and then takes her things off again. She doesn't express what she herself wants, though the fact that she writes of these offers makes one believe Mercy would have liked to take her uncle up on them.

Staying for the winter would be something different, an opportunity away from Prince Edward Island, where she likely knew everyone, every bachelor, every possible match open to her. In Bloomfield, she'd have a much wider selection of possible mates, even if they were first cousins. Her parents, however, didn't want her to stay, and, surprisingly, that was the end of that.

Her parents were emphatic about her not staying for the winter, and "would not hear of it." It could have been they were worried about her health. They'd taken care with her education and perhaps they thought Bloomfield would be too rural a life for her and would not offer enough opportunities, in life or for marriage. This is speculation though. Mercy gives no indication of why her parents say no.

Mercy herself perhaps felt vulnerable after having been so sick, and was still not fully recovered. Life in Ohio would have been quite different, too — there were no servants, and it was a more rural existence. Maybe she didn't want to stay, but she does sound disappointed. Even something as simple as going out for a walk with her uncle is quashed because her father feels it is too damp outside. This shows that her parents were still concerned for her health, but it also shows Mercy's willingness to be directed by her parents. She is following the expectations society placed on young unmarried women.

One wishes Mercy would have spoken up, said what she wanted, or at least made it clear in her diary. We want all her intelligence and her insight to be directed at herself. Writing a diary, in and of itself, shows a degree of independence, with one free to write personal thoughts, and Mercy had done so before. It would have been good if she had done so again. But it's still 1864, and generally, women didn't speak up, or have ambitions upon which they could act freely. The general approach to life was for a woman to subsume herself in her husband's life. The aim was to marry. Even today, in the twenty-first century, one could argue that Western culture, with its emphasis on the princess as a role model for young girls, can tend to promote marriage and the domestic "epic" as the best of a woman's life choices.

Nevertheless, the diary stands as a testament to a young woman's need to present and preserve a life. Mercy Coles kept writing, even while desperately ill. She maintained and preserved the original diary throughout her life. Likely all the mementos and "cartes" of her time at the conference events and tour of the Canadas on this momentous six-week journey that her obituary mentions were kept by her family, at least for a time. Mercy Coles recognized her diary as important, worthy of posterity. The diary is representative of, and a testament to, a young unmarried woman's life and views at a seminal point in Canada's history. It is, as well, of course, the only Canadian female account of the Confederation events.

Mercy must have wanted to marry. She gave every indication she was interested in the men she met, and commented on their looks, their behaviour, and their attention toward her. Five weeks had gone by since Mercy and her parents left Prince Edward Island on October 5; time and opportunity for Mercy to be wooed were running out.

## *Thirteen*

# Going Home

*Thursday, November 10 to Thursday, November 17*

The 1860s was the age of awe, the age of enthrallment at what humankind could create, at what it could do. The world was on a fast-paced and heady journey of progress, from Farini's and Blondin's tightrope walks over Niagara Falls,* to Montreal's Victoria Bridge, and from Notman's new

* The French acrobat Charles Blondin is better-known to history, but the Great Farini — William Hunt of Port Hope, Ontario — was by far the better businessman and had greater success at making a living with his acrobatic feats. There was a rivalry between the two acrobats in the early 1860s at Niagara Falls, and they each tried to outdo the other in various tricks — crossing a tightrope blindfolded, or with their feet in sacks. They carried tables, stoves, and washing tubs on their backs, and stopped midway to use them. Blondin made an omelette, and lowered it down to the *Maid of the Mist*. In Farini's case, he lowered himself down to the boat, and climbed back up again. Blondin carried his agent across, piggyback style.

and brilliant photography, to Tom Thumb and Barnum's "wonders" that "would take [Mercy] a week to think of it all," she wrote.

The 1860s were similar to the 1960s in their leap away from the past — not just a moving forward, but a way of life completely different from what had come before, from the way things *used* to be. Even the Civil War was considered "new." Often referred to as the first "modern" war, with its new style of guns and bullets designed in the 1860s, its powerful artillery — the machinery that caused mass destruction of land and infrastructure — and the many killed, the war was fundamentally different in many ways from those that had been fought just a few decades previously.

Here in Canada, political union and the forming of a real country was finally about to happen. The railway was creating a democracy of movement; travel was affordable, and much of the country, previously inaccessible, was now possible to journey through. The world was new. What a time to be young, what a time to start. Even if you were a still-youngish, still-unmarried woman.

The Coles family began their return trip home on Thursday, November 10. Mercy Coles and her parents left their relatives and travelled onwards, touring through New York City and Boston before they began the final leg of the trip home. New York City was then as alluring and full of entertainment as we think of it today.

All this was undertaken as the Civil War still raged. Sherman's final destruction of Atlanta began on November 12, leaving the city a smoking ruin. New York City was nearly burned to the ground; one of the fires started next to a theatre on Broadway, where John Wilkes Booth was performing. People were enthralled with Tom Thumb and in awe of Broadway — no one seemed to have a worry or a care in the world, least of all any concern over the Civil War.

---

Farini seemed to recognize the importance of the Confederation talks, and while the Fathers met in Quebec, he offered to wheel the governor general, Lord Monck, across a tightrope over Montmorency Falls. Farini's biographer, Shane Peacock, reports that Monck agreed, but in the end the powers that be wouldn't allow a line to be strung across the falls. There are no other reports of Farini cavorting with the delegates, or dallying with their lives. Mercy doesn't mention Farini anywhere in her diary.

Meanwhile, Mercy was hoping to see Leonard Tilley again, before it all ended, before her father became set against Confederation … before he went mad, before she became too old.

But first —

As they began their journey back to PEI, Mercy wrote that they had lunch in the eating saloon, "the first she was ever in," at the train station, because her Uncle William wanted them to. By Mercy's standards, this was unusual, and yet upper-class Feo Monck often ate at train stations. On October 6, 1864, Feo wrote, "The dinners you get at railway stations in Canada are so much better than what you get when you are travelling at home." The food may have been good, but the travelling wasn't. On her return trip from Niagara Falls, October 13, Feo wrote:

> None of the trains this side of the Atlantic *connect*, so we had to wait every now and then an hour, or more, and they are always after their time. I know nothing more irritating than travelling in this country — what with the trains missing "connection," and the spitting and beastliness. We had a very good dinner at Hamilton — roast beef, potatoes and butter, cabbage, apple pie, beer and cheese. I give you our bill of fare to show how much more civilized the food is than what you get in civilized England, where you rush in at stations to get old and cold soup, and horrid sandwiches.

Mercy and Feo also both travelled in sleeping cars. The famous Pullman sleeping car was released in April 1864, but neither Mercy's nor Feo's descriptions sound like they travelled in the new luxury cars. They both write similar accounts of their travel conditions, which speak of how accessible train travel was to all and sundry. Mercy writes that she and her mother were "first up" when they have a sleeping car, and thus they get the "clean towel." On her trip back from Niagara Falls, Feo continues:

> At Toronto we "embarked aboard the sleeping cars" where they can't spit much because there is matting, and they are not allowed. We were more comfortable than the others, as no one was allowed to sleep over us.... and then they [a newlywed couple] went to bed, and oh! that was a horrid sight. Off went the man's coat, waistcoat, braces, and boots, and then they tucked themselves into bed. We had no curtains and only cloaks for bedclothes, so we were lucky; but these wretches tucked the curtains all round them. Ugh!

On the way to New York, Mercy and her parents travelled through the new oil cities of Corry and Meadville, Pennsylvania. Oil was big, and there was quick money to be made — and lost. The brothers of John Wilkes Booth pleaded with him to stop his speculating for oil, to forget about politics, and return to his acting career with them. On November 25, less than two weeks after Mercy attended a performance at the Broadway theater, managed by Edwin Booth, the three Booth brothers, Edwin, John Wilkes, and Junius Brutus Booth, Jr., performed together for the first and only time, in a one-night performance of *Julius Caesar*, as a fundraiser for a statue of Shakespeare in Central Park.*

Just an hour into the show, Confederates set fire to the city, including the house that adjoined the theatre. The theatre was packed, and the crowd began to panic. The *New York Times* reported the fires as "one of the most fiendish and inhuman acts known in modern times." Edwin Booth, anticipating a chaotic mass exodus, stepped out of character — he was playing the role of Brutus — and calmed the crowd. In the end, the theatre was saved, and so was the city. It was only five months later that his brother John Wilkes Booth assassinated Abraham Lincoln.

General William T. Sherman of the Northern states, for Lincoln's Union government, took Atlanta in September 1864. It was this event that helped Lincoln beat George McClellan in the election on November 8. Before Sherman left on his famous March to the Sea, he had Atlanta destroyed. On November 12, he ordered the business district ruined. Over the next few

* The statue is still there.

days, the city was razed. There are numerous eyewitness accounts, including his own, of how complete, and how terrible, it was. Sherman's military secretary, Henry Hitchcock, who had only just joined Sherman's forces the month before, wrote on November 15:

> Today the destruction fairly commenced.... First bursts of smoke, dense, black volumes, then tongues of flame, then huge waves of fire roll up into the sky: presently the skeletons of great warehouses stand out in relief against and amidst sheets of roaring, blazing, furious flames, — then the angry waves roll less high, and are of deeper color, then sink and cease, and only the fierce glow from the bare and blackened walls ... as one fire sinks another rises, further along the horizon ... it is a line of fire and smoke, lurid, angry, dreadful to look upon.

Sherman, ever a general, gives an account that is a mixed bag of ruin and elation:

> About 7 a.m. of November 16th we rode out of Atlanta by the Decatur road, filled by the marching troops and wagons of the Fourteenth Corps; and reaching the hill, just outside of the old rebel works, we naturally paused to look back upon the scenes of our past battles. We stood upon the very ground whereon was fought the bloody battle of July 22d and could see the copse of wood where McPherson fell. Behind us lay Atlanta, smoldering and in ruins, the black smoke rising high in air and hanging like a pall over the ruined city.... Then we turned our horses' heads to the east; Atlanta was soon lost behind the screen of trees, and became a thing of the past. Around it clings many a thought of desperate battle, of hope and fear, that now seem like the memory of a dream. The day was extremely beautiful, clear sunlight, with bracing air, and an unusual feeling of exhilaration seemed to pervade

> all minds — a feeling of something to come, vague and undefined, still full of venture and intense interest.

On the ship from Boston to New Brunswick, on Tuesday, November 15, Mercy met a Mr. Solomon and his wife, who were fleeing Atlanta. Nothing about the meeting could possibly convey the horrors of the destruction of Atlanta — either Mercy's writing, or the cavalier way Mr. Solomon behaved. One might guess why Mercy wrote in the fashion she did. As a youngish woman wanting to be wooed, hoping for romance, or at least a viable marriage, her job, her aim was to be bright and airy, the way she wanted life to be, as though life were nothing more than the pursuit of pleasure. But how different is that from today? It's the prerogative of the young, this lighthearted look at life, regardless of the era.

Mr. Solomon, of course, was behaving as a Southern gentleman would. It wouldn't be right or proper to speak of the war in any real fashion with a young woman. Even though troops at the front were able to read the newspapers within two days of their publication, the war would not be commonplace or suitable for public discussion with women.

In Saint John, at the hotel, on November 15, with Mr. Solomon, Mercy writes that they sang the "Bonnie Blue Flag" again. One can't imagine this would be the Southern Confederate version, after just having come from her uncle's. Nor, presumably, would Mr. Solomon have been singing a Union song, although it is possible Mr. Solomon was a Union supporter, even though he was from the South. The aims of both the North and the South were viewed positively at different times in Prince Edward Island. Some Islanders were worried about what the North might do when the war ended, but there was sympathy for the South's right to self-determination. George Coles had expressed support for the South, too, though that was in 1861. Thus, Mercy may have known both Union and Confederate versions of the song. Here, again, the Civil War plays foil to Mercy Coles's trip away from home.

Mercy Coles wasn't concerned with writing for posterity. The importance of her writing stems from the fact that it was written in that exact moment in time, when the things she wrote about were in the process of happening, before they became important events of interest. And so, there is no purposeful excluding, or including, of information. Everything Mercy thought of importance or interest is here. History is usually dictated from the viewpoint of the victors — in this case, the men who had position and power. With Mercy Coles's diary, we have the rare opportunity to look back through the eyes of a young, single woman at the events, the time, and the men of this pivotal point in the history of both Canada and the United States.

The style and intent of the writer affect our reading of the material, of course. Knowing what we know now of the past, and of Mercy, she sometimes comes across as too blithe, too innocent. Mr. Solomon might have written of this episode differently, as would George Coles. Mercy's intent may be to be cheery, light, but the fact that this is a diary, presumably meant for herself, and possibly her family's enjoyment, too, means one expects more — more insight, more knowledge, more understanding. Mercy has proven to be a keen observer of people and their behaviour. Again, one wishes Mercy would speak directly to the times, the women, the men, and about herself. She has given us a great glimpse of what she *could* tell us. George Brown's assessment of Mercy and her sisters makes us believe there is more to Mercy than what we have here, near the end of her journey. Really, we *want* more, because we know there *is* more.

Mercy Coles's hopes that Leonard Tilley will be thinking of her, and her wish to see him again, as well as her later writing of how her uncle thinks she is "perfect" and "suited [her uncle] in every way" perhaps signifies here, at the end of her journey, a questioning of herself, of her identity, of the identity she has been creating. Why *had* she stopped being the object of Tilley's attention, and perhaps others'? She desires to please, and is happy her uncle finds her "perfect." She discloses insecurity in her search for approval, now that the conference and potential for being wooed are at an end. Mercy doesn't quibble with the expectations of her as a single young woman when her parents deny her the option to stay at her uncle's, overnight or all winter. She is willing to live by the conventions expected of her, and does not appear to chafe at the limitations. Earlier, during the conference and tour, Mercy behaved more flirtatiously, teasing and being teased, taking fancies to different men, enjoying the attention she received. Her diary now reflects how a young woman is expected to view and approach life, and how she should perceive herself; it has a more conventional tone, one tied to Victorian ideals.

The Americans have collected a significant amount of primary source material on the Civil War. In comparison, Canadians have very little direct source material — a miniscule amount — on the making of Confederation. George Brown's letters to his wife, Anne, written during the Confederation conferences, evocative with revealing personal and political detail; Feo Monck's unedited journal; and Marcy Coles's diary are the only first-person, not intended for publication, private accounts we have that chronicle the social side of the events and the impact they had on the crucial relationship building that went on during the Confederation conferences. The Brown letters were only discovered in the 1950s. The Mercy Coles diary is equally important to our understanding of Confederation, the time, and our relationship with the United States at this volatile period.

*November 10, Thursday [en route from Warren, Ohio, to New York City]*
Atlantic and Great Western. We left Warren at 12 o'clock. Uncle and Aunt Haine and George Dunkerton came down to the station with us. We went out shopping with Aunt after breakfast. We had luncheon in the eating saloon. The first I ever was in, it was rather a strange place. Uncle would have us go, so to please him we went. He is a dear old man and petted me to [accept? unclear]. We are to travel all day and all night. We will get in to [unclear] tomorrow morning. [unclear] brought me some cartes of the children. Uncle and [wife?] are going to have Papa's [unclear] and send them to us. We stayed at Meadville a ½ an hour for dinner. Neither Ma nor I got out for we were not hungry. We are now at Corry [Pennsylvania] the great city for oil. They are building everywhere. There is an [muse? unclear] building just east of where the barrel of oil. Such a splendid lot of oil they run 1500 barrels of oil a day. Making money as fast as they do in California. At Meadville there was a splendid Hotel right at the Station. Pa says it is the finest he has seen in America. I have just had such a nice sleep! We do not get a sleeping car until we stop at Jamestown. Ma and I will then go to bed and sleep well I hope.

9 o'clock We stopt at Salamanca and had tea. It is a beautiful moonlight night so I think we may safely up to bed. Papa has secured us a berth in the sleeping car and we are going to bed about 10 o'clock. I wonder if Uncle William has got home. He told Papa I was perfect, suited him every way.

*Friday morning, November 11th [still en route to New York City]*
Ma and I had a good safe sleep in the berth. Lucky we had no person but ourselves. We got up as soon as it was daylight and washed our things. We were first and had the clean towel. Pa to [unclear] stopping all through the night at every stopping place. We expect to get into New York at 1 o'clock. We have just seen the place where the train ran over a bridge last [Sun?]day night and killed 5 people. One [?] of the cars are still there.

*St. Nicolas Hotel, New York, ½ past 2*
We arrived here about ½ an hour ago and our trunks have not yet appeared, it is no use grumbling for you do not know who to scold. We are [near?] Broadway such a busy place everybody rushing about. We got into a cab when we arrived at the Station and were driven on board the Ferry boat and did not get out until we were set down at this door. Such a long tunnel we came through just before we got out of the train.

*Saturday, November 12 [en route from NYC to Boston, Massachusetts]*
On board the Metropolis [Fall?] liner.

We left New York at 3 o'clock. Such a morning as we had walking and driving the whole time. Yesterday we went wherever we [desired?]. Off to Barnum's. Tom Thumb and his wife are in Europe but we saw five other dwarfs, 2 albino children with perfectly white hair, such lots of wonders it wd take me a week to think of it all. There was a girl there only 16 years of age with her arms as big around as my waist. She is rather pretty. In the evening we went to the Broadway Theater and saw Owen act [Solon?] Shanghai. It was capital. We have just been introduced to a Mr. [Cumming?], a gentleman from Boston. He is just telling Papa that the Perlys are great friends of his. This morning we went shopping. We bought photograph albums for Loo and Mary. Feathers for them too. A *Ladies Companion* for Gina, boots for the boys.* The ladies are certainly the best dressed I ever saw. Nothing but diamonds, every lady at the tables at the St. Nicolas had a diamond ring on her finger. This morning we drove quite to the head of 5th Avenue. There is the most magnificent residence anybody ever saw, such a pretty Episcopal Church the [ivy?] growing all over it. We have been having a race with the [? name of ship]. She [unclear] us at first but the *Metropolis* got up her steam and soon got ahead of her. This Steamer is a regular floating palace, all white paint and gilt. The [unclear] is the whole length of the steamer from bow to stern. Ma has gone to bed. I must follow [unclear].

*Nov 13th / 64, Sunday, Lemont House, Boston*

We arrived here this morning about ½ past 4. We arrived at Newport at 4. We met a Mr. Cummings on board the Steamer and he got Papa to take tickets for a Pars[?] carriage. It was a splendid affair. The worst of it was we never looked in just as they do in England.** This seems a very nice hotel. Unfortunately it is raining so I am afraid we shall not see much of the city. We did not see a

* Mercy is referring to her sisters Louisa and Mary Victoria, twenty and seventeen years old respectively, and Georgianna, twenty-two years old, and married a year already. The boys are her brothers, Russell and Charlie, nine and five years old.

** These are the words, but it's not at all clear what Mercy means.

[unclear] of New York we knew. I thought the Porter was D'Arcy.* He looked exactly like him.

Papa has been to the [Lemont?] House.** The Grays and Popes left there last Thursday. They wd be home last night. He did not ask if the Tuppers were there [now?] [Unclear — Likely?] they were for they all left [Niagara?] together. We have just come in from an hour's drive which cost $5. Boston is certainly a very pretty place. The Commons in summer must be splendid. Our driver under took showing us the sights. Chester Park is very pretty, rows of trees fenced in, in the centre of the streets. Very handsome residences on each side. I think it is quite as nice as 5th Avenue in New York. The business part of the town is not so [unclear] as Broadway but there are some very handsome buildings. We saw a block built by a Mr. [Bahee?], very handsome shops. I shd liked to have gone to church but it is snowing so hard on the [unclear]. We leave tomorrow morning for St. John New Brunswick in the Steamer. I hope we shall have a day in St. John but I am afraid not.

*Monday afternoon, November 14*
*[en route from Boston to Portland, Maine]*
On board the *New Brunswick*. We left Boston this morning at [2?] o'clock. I had not been on board many minutes before I had to [unclear] my bed and here I have been ever since. I have been very seasick. All hands have gone to dinner. I could not bear to go below. The Stewardess gave me some soup for lunch, but it came up directly.

*November 15th, Tuesday evening*
*[en route from Portland to Saint John, New Brunswick]*
I got up and went on shore at Portland to get my tea last night.

* Does she mean D'Arcy McGee?

** The hotel name looks the same as the name of the hotel the Coles are staying at.

When we came on board again I thought I saw a face I knew and who should it be but [John?]. He was as pleased to see us as we were to see him. He has just come from Quebec and has been from the Island for 3 weeks. I am in the wheel house writing. I slept so poorly last night, we heard that something in [very/every?] [unclear]. We get to [?]port. All the rest of our party went down in this same boat last week. We will not get into St John tonight until 9 o'clock. *I wonder if we shall see Mr. Tilley* [emphasis mine]. The Steeves are home.

*Stubbs Hotel, Saint John, NB*
We arrived here at 8 o'clock. We met such a nice man on board the Steamer, Mr. Solomon and his wife of South Carolina [likely she means Georgia]. They were at Atlanta when Sherman captured it. Their house was shelled and they were ordered to depart. He gave me a 10 dollar note. I am to keep it until it is worth its equivalent in gold. Uncle William gave me a 100 dollar one but Mr. Solomon says it is forgery. Mr. Eckhart and Mr. Solomon are taking a glass of brandy and water with Papa. I found a note here from Mr. Tilley with his copies of the photographs of St. Peter's on the Island. He says they had a very pleasant trip down. He encloses a pass for us to go over the railway free. We started off to Mr. Manson's the moment we arrived and bought Eliza* a bonnet. The shop was shut but we rapped at the door and they opened the door, ½ past 10. I have just written to Mr. Tilley to thank him for his pass.**

* Mercy's sister, twenty-four years old, and about to be married in December.

** Then there is a short line at the bottom of the page that is too faint to read. Too bad, as it may have provided a little more insight into Mercy's feelings about Leonard Tilley.

*November 16th, Wednesday afternoon [en route from Saint John to Shediac, NB, by train, and Shediac to Charlottetown, PEI, by ship]* We left St John this morning at 8.* We arrived at Shediac at 2 [or 12?]. There we found James Duncan, John Yeo and Louis [Lewis] Carvell.** Quite an addition to our party. Mr. Carvell has given me his carte and we have been chatting ever since we came on board. He thinks he will probably remain in the Island all winter. We expect to get to Summerside in a few minutes. I have not been the least seasick. I did not see Mr. Solomon this morning. We sang "Bonnie Blue Flag" last night before we went to bed.*** We are nearly home. The light was not lit on St. Peter's Island and we have gone about 12 miles out of our way. We will not get to the wharf until after 11 instead of a few minutes after 10. I have had nothing to eat since breakfast so will be well prepared for my supper. I expect they will be tired waiting for us. I have been sitting about chatting with Mr. Carvell for four hours, Mr. Eckhart occasionally joining in the conversation. He is a very nice man and I have had a very pleasant conversation.

And there ends the diary. *Pleasant.* A good word, and a completely impossible word to sum up this hopeful and fantastic journey of Confederation — a journey aiming for a future, intending a future, for her, for her province, for the politicians wanting a bigger, broader life of their own, and for the country that would be.

---

* They would have been travelling on the train, using the free pass Leonard Tilley had left them at the hotel.

** James Duncan was a shipbuilder; John Yeo was a Conservative in the PEI legislature, son of shipbuilder James Yeo; and Lewis Carvell was the younger brother of businessman Jedediah Slason Carvell.

*** They were at the Stubbs Hotel, in Saint John. One wonders which version of the "Bonnie Blue Flag" they sang. If Mr. Solomon were a Confederate, he wouldn't be singing the Union version, nor does it seem likely Mercy would be singing the Confederate version.

Some got what they wanted. Canada, finally, by 1867, had become a country. John A. Macdonald became its first prime minister. He did marry again; he married his former secretary Hewitt Bernard's sister, Agnes Bernard, a strong woman who helped keep him more sober and healthier than he might have been otherwise. The politicians who'd remained pro-Confederation became ministers in Macdonald's new federal government. Charles Tupper even became prime minister for a while, a short while. Leonard Tilley was a minister in Macdonald's government for eighteen years, and was lieutenant-governor of New Brunswick twice, the second term ending in 1893. He remarried in 1867, to a twenty-three-year-old woman, eight months younger than his eldest son. But Edward Whelan died in 1867, D'Arcy McGee was assassinated in 1868, and William Pope left government after his anti-Confederation brother, James Pope, became premier of PEI. (James Pope was premier when PEI did finally join Confederation in 1873, but that may have had more to do with the railroad, and how important it was to him, than with any nationalist feeling.) William Pope continued to fight for Confederation on PEI, until the Island, on the brink of bankruptcy because of the railway, finally joined Canada. Colonel Gray of PEI left politics, too, at the end of 1864, when PEI didn't join Confederation. And George Coles turned completely against Confederation when the offer of money to buy out the Island's absentee landlords and resolve the land question was dropped.

More than that, Coles, though he was premier again by 1867, resigned his seat in August 1868 because his mind was deteriorating. He was thought to be mad, and had first been locked up in his own house, then admitted to the New Brunswick Lunatic Asylum in June 1869 for two years. He came home again, but got worse, and was placed in the Prince Edward Island asylum by June of 1871. Not only were methods of treating mental illness at the time draconian and of limited use, but the Island's asylum was also in terrible shape. It was described as "worse than the Black Hole of Calcutta." By the summer of 1869, Coles's wife had to ask that his business affairs be taken away from him, and the committee in charge of it discovered his debts were greater than his assets. His brewery business was put up for sale, as well as a number of properties, in order to maintain his family; six of Coles's children were still at home, including Mercy. Mercy's mother, as well as

Mercy's two young brothers, her sister Mary Victoria (until she married in 1871), and her only other unmarried sister, Alexandrina Octavia, continued to live at Stone Park Farm until 1875, when it was sold.

While he was locked away, George Coles wrote that he was worried his family would starve to death. On September 14, 1873, he wrote: "Stone Farm House Locked in a Bed room / Deserted by God & Man / The Miserable and Unfortunate / Hon. George Coles." Coles died on August 21, 1875. He never regained his sanity. For the man who had achieved responsible government for Prince Edward Island and established the Free Education Act, it was a sad and sorry finish.

And Mercy Coles? Mercy never did marry. She lived to be eighty-three years old. Her father's insanity can't have helped her case. Her youngest sister, Octavia Alexandrina, who was fifteen years younger than Mercy, didn't marry either. In Mercy Coles's obituary, in the Charlottetown *Guardian* on February 12, 1921, it says, "She was a recognized authority on the early history of the province and indeed of Canada." She'd kept all her mementos of her journey to Quebec, such as the dance cards of which she writes, "filled out by [the men] themselves," and the photo "cartes" she'd received. Her obituary notes that the friendships she'd made with the famous Fathers continued, but now she'd survived them all.

Aside from the "Extracts of a Diary" in the Charlottetown *Guardian* of 1917, and the obituary notice in 1921, not much more is known of Mercy Coles's life. There are two final travel diaries held by Library and Archives Canada (LAC). The main one covers a trip in August 1878 (George Coles would have been dead three years) to Montreal with her sister Alexandrina and her mother. Mercy was forty, her sister was twenty-five, and her mother sixty-one years old. Mercy writes of the places and things they saw; it is a typical travel diary, interesting as a travelogue, but with little of historical note in it.

As to personal matters, it's clear Mercy may still have had hopes for marriage. Her sister Alexandrina must certainly have had. Mercy writes, "There are a great many passengers on board, *some very nice looking gentlemen* [emphasis mine]. I have got mother in my stateroom. Drina takes a Miss Randall who is going to Halifax. The Head Steward made as much fuss over our coming back as if we belonged to him."

The second travel diary is from 1879, covering a trip to New Brunswick, and the LAC version is only two pages long. Both diaries are quite difficult to decipher, though the 1878 one is clear in parts.

Mercy outlived both her brothers and all her sisters, except for Alexandrina, who died in 1927. Her mother passed away in 1893. In the 1881 PEI census, Mercy, Alexandrina, and their mother are listed as living with Mercy's brother Charles, who, at twenty-two years of age, was listed as "head of the household."

In Mercy's obituary, the *Guardian* further says, "[She was] an estimable lady, friendly, sociable, charitable and intellectually brilliant." In her later diaries, she returns to her vivacious self, commenting on the behaviour of others, and the gentlemen they met on their trips. Perhaps Mercy was speculating on possible matches there could be for her or her sister when she wrote of the "nice looking gentlemen." We will give the last, "pleasant" word to Mercy. Her 1878 travel diary ends here:

> What a delightful time we had. I never enjoyed myself more, we never heard a cross word or saw a black look. I shall always remember my trip on the *Miramichi* as a bright spot in my life.

*Fourteen*

# Confederation Suitors

And what of Mercy's Confederation suitors? Why weren't any of the possible matches successful? What became of them, and why didn't things work out?

Whether John A. Macdonald was only paying attention to Mercy for political expediency can't be known. He definitely did disappear, either into drink or because he was ill, at the end of the Quebec conference and for the tour of Canada. He went to Toronto, but didn't appear at any of the functions or meetings. He wrote later that he'd been ill. He did go back to Prince Edward Island in later years, with Agnes. In 1917, Mercy says that he'd "always proved a very kind friend" to her. But how likely would it have been that Macdonald would have seriously considered Mercy as a mate when she'd been away, deathly sick, for two weeks of the conference? After suffering through the long, long illnesses of his first wife, Isabella, how much would he, or could he, really let himself fall for someone who was so sick? At 138 pounds, Mercy was no waif like Isabella, but she may have appeared too young, too fragile for Macdonald to consider her as a potential mate. And, of course, George Coles's decided turn against Confederation wouldn't have helped Mercy's case, either.

Macdonald married Agnes Bernard in February 1867. They had one daughter in 1869, Mary, who was born with hydrocephalus. Her father doted on her, and she ended up living until 1933, a fairly long life for a person in her circumstances. Agnes, who was thirty-one when she married the fifty-two-year-old John A., outlived him by twenty-nine years.

That nothing progressed between Mercy and another Maritimer like herself, Leonard Tilley, is perhaps saddest of all. He had seemed genuinely interested in Mercy Coles, and she in him, not that she spoke as gaily of him as she did of Macdonald, or as flirtatiously as she did of Hewitt Bernard. In the main, she spoke of him in a way that made him sound like a viable prospect. Tilley did go on to remarry, in 1867; a young woman, not a mature forty-year-old like Mrs. Alexander. So, Mercy, at twenty-six years, would have been a much more likely contender for Leonard Tilley's affections than Mrs. Alexander. Alice Starr Chipman was only twenty-three years old when she married Tilley, and was the daughter of a friend of his. He went on to have two more children with her, and they lived a seemingly happy life together. Tilley lived till he was seventy-eight, and died June 25, 1896, of blood poisoning from a cut he'd gotten on his foot. There is no record of further connection between Mercy Coles and Leonard Tilley after the Confederation conferences, aside from the information in the *Guardian* that says Mercy maintained a friendship with him, as well as with "several other personages ... distinguished in the history of Canada."

Again, though, politics likely influenced Tilley's ideas of who an appropriate mate might be. Tilley was pro-Confederation, and went to the polls only four months after the Quebec conference. He lost that election, and even lost his own seat. It would hardly have been the time to be courting the daughter (or sister, in the case of Mrs. Alexander) of the men now so set against Confederation as George Coles or Thomas Haviland were.

Hewitt Bernard, the secretary of the conference, appeared to be another serious contender as a suitor for Mercy. He also had the potential to be less affected by political motives, as he was not voting on the resolutions, nor representing any political party. As well, at thirty-nine, he was the youngest of these three possible suitors. Mercy writes of Hewitt Bernard having gout: "He looks awful. I tease him about it, it is a great shame but I can't help it."

Hewitt Bernard in 1862.

The relationship could be seen as flirtatious and intimate, or brotherly, but it seems more of a flirtatious nature, especially since she starts off her journal saying, "Major Bernard tells me we are to have good times.... The first word almost he said was, 'I hope you brought the irresistible blue silk.'" Mercy is taken with the time, looking forward to events, and definitely enjoying the compliments and attention. All through the weeks of the conference and tour, she writes of how Hewitt Bernard calls on her every day. She's disappointed when he comes to dinner with her family but she is away sick. And she can't stop herself from teasing him.

Hewitt Bernard never married, either. He lived in Ottawa, once it was declared the capital, even though he disliked it intensely, calling it a "hot, dusty, fifth rate little Peddlington." Once John A. Macdonald and Bernard's sister, Agnes, were married in 1867, he lived with them in Ottawa. He was the deputy judge advocate general of Canada West, and then became Canada's first deputy minister of justice in 1867. His plate was full with the work his position entailed. And the gout he had during the conference plagued him his whole life. He probably had rheumatoid arthritis; it eventually crippled him. He had to resign by the time he was fifty-one, in 1876, and ended up an invalid. In the winter, he took to living in a sanatorium in New Jersey. When Hewitt visited with the Macdonalds, Agnes would go for walks with her brother, Hewitt, in one wheelchair and her daughter, Mary, in another. Hewitt Bernard died in 1893, at sixty-eight years of age: no doubt his rheumatoid arthritis shortened his life.

Charles Drinkwater, John A. Macdonald's private secretary, also called on Mercy every day when she was ill. He brought her a bouquet for the first event. But Drinkwater was only twenty-one years old. Still, it was common enough then for women to marry men close to their own age, though he was five years younger than Mercy. He would have been well enough off with his position. In his photograph, taken by William Notman in 1866, he does sport a small goatee and moustache, but has no sideburns — the clean-faced kind of look Mercy seems to have appreciated. Nevertheless, though we hear of him calling on her, and bringing bouquets to her, we don't hear much more of him. We don't hear about whether he's made sure to dance with her, and she never talks of teasing him. We don't learn much at all about him through Mercy.

Drinkwater was born in England, and worked for the railway until he became John A. Macdonald's secretary. He returned to the railway later in his life, and became the first secretary of the Canadian Pacific Railway. The town of Drinkwater, Saskatchewan (more or less between Moose Jaw and Rouleau*) is named after him. He married the daughter of Duncan Graham in 1868.

Nothing more is known of Mr. Crowther, Alexander Galt's secretary, of whom Mercy writes: "Mr. Crowther is here. He came to call on me this morning. He wants to hold me good for the dance I promised him at Quebec." Also, "I feel quite well this morning. I went down to the Ball last night. Such a splendid affair. Mr. Crowther danced with me the first Quadrille." Crowther also called on Mercy every day when she was away sick. As is the case with the women, not as much information can be found on the less "distinguished" men as on those who already were so, or became so in time.

Even the final conversation of which Mercy writes in her diary, the four-hour chat with Lewis Carvell, seems promising. But Carvell, at thirty-six, had been married sixteen years already, and had four children. He helped his brother Jedediah Slason Carvell run his very successful import and export business, Carvell Brothers, in Prince Edward Island. Jedediah had moved from New Brunswick to Charlottetown only recently in 1860. He was pro-Confederation, and had married a niece of Leonard Tilley's first wife, Julia Hanford. Lewis Carvell, his wife, and some of his children moved at some point to Charlottetown, but they're buried in New Brunswick.

* Rouleau is better known as Dog River in the television show *Corner Gas.*

Charles Drinkwater in Montreal, 1866. Charles Drinkwater visited Mercy Coles every day when she was ill. Drinkwater was John A. Macdonald's secretary, and was twenty-one years old at the Quebec conference.

*Fifteen*

# Daughters and Fathers

Meanwhile, one wonders what happened to all those other "Daughters of Confederation." As the unmarried daughters and sisters of the delegates went along to the Quebec conference largely to (let's face it) meet potential husbands among the unmarried men of the rest of the country, it would be interesting to know whether they succeeded.

Ten young women, nine of whom were from the Maritimes, went to Quebec City, and on the tour of the Canadas, in October 1864. Their fate afterward is something that is difficult to trace. In some instances, in which there was more than one daughter of marriageable age in a family, one can only make a best-guess estimate of who went on the trip, based on the ages of all the sisters. The women from Prince Edward Island were Mercy Coles, Margaret Gray, and Mary Alice Brecken Haviland Alexander. From Nova Scotia, there was Emma Tupper, daughter of Charles Tupper, and Joanna Archibald, daughter of Adams Archibald. Four of the single young women came from New Brunswick; there were two of William Steeves's daughters — likely Caroline Steeves and either Lucinda, Henrietta, or Martha. Also from New Brunswick was Charlotte Elizabeth Gray, daughter of Colonel

John Hamilton Gray; and Jane Fisher, daughter of Charles Fisher. Jessie McDougall, daughter of William McDougall, was the only young woman from Canada who was present in Quebec City.

Researching women's history is no easy task. Mercy herself never recorded the first names of the other young women with her (except for once, when she wrote that the doctor told her that his daughter Emma was sick). Often, information on a father makes very little reference, if any, to his children, particularly female children. Here is the listing for Colonel John Hamilton Gray of PEI, from the *Dictionary of Canadian Biography*, as an example:

> [S]oldier and politician; b. 14 June 1811 at Charlottetown, P.E.I; … m. first Susan Pennefather (d. 1866), and they had at least two children [Gray had *five* daughters with Susan Pennefather]; m. secondly in 1869 Sarah Caroline Cambridge, and they had three children; d. 13 Aug. 1887 at Charlottetown.

If a list of children can be found, often the daughters' names are overwritten by their husbands' names, for example, as "Mrs. Alfred Seymour" as in the case of William McDougall's daughter, Jessie. One then has to find out who Alfred Seymour is in order to find the first name of his wife, and then discover whether she, as an unmarried woman, went along for the Confederation talks and tour.

Prince Edward Island's Colonel Gray's daughter Margaret was interviewed by the *Halifax Herald* seventy-three years after the Confederation talks in Charlottetown, and the September 1, 1937, *Winnipeg Free Press* reported on the article. Under the title "She Saw Canada Born," the article opens with:

> Down in Prince Edward Island resides the last living link with that historic moment in Canada's life — the Quebec Conference of 1864 — which laid the plans for a united Dominion. That person is the 92 year young [she was nineteen during the Confederation talks] Mrs. Artemus Lord, daughter of Colonel John H. Gray. She heard the Fathers of Confederation plan a Canada that would extend from sea to sea.…

> In the summer of 1864, says the *Halifax Herald*, Miss Gray had been visiting in Halifax and it was just after her return that the Nova Scotia delegates arrived in Charlottetown to confer with the Islanders and to pick them up so they could all travel together to Quebec.*
>
> Among the delegates was Dr. Charles Tupper, and with him were Mrs. Tupper, and their pretty daughter Emma. Dr. Tupper was attracted by his friend's lively daughter, and asked: "Col. Gray, why don't you bring your daughter to Quebec?"
>
> "Too late now," smiled Col. Gray, looking at his great silver watch. "We have only 15 minutes before we start for the dock."
>
> "Well, my dear," said Mrs. Gray [who didn't go because she was quite sick and would die within two years], "if you'll take her, I'll get her ready before the boat sails."

There is something wrong about this story, regarding the dates, and what happened when; nevertheless, it's an interesting bit to add about another one of the "Daughters of Confederation." There is little more of substance added by this article — we don't even find out the woman's first name — but we may be able to infer a bit about the dynamics at work during the social events.

For example, it might say something about Charles Tupper and his "attractions." In *1867*, Moore writes, "He [Tupper] was married for sixty-five years, and friends insisted the marriage was happy and close, but letters — vanished now from Tupper's papers but preserved in [John] Thompson's — suggest a Tupper who was aggressively sexual."** Sandra Gwyn's *The Private Capital* also contends Tupper had relations with women

---

* Of course, the group did not actually travel to Quebec until October, and the Charlottetown conference was at the beginning of September, so somebody has something not quite right here.

** Moore, on page 34, is referencing Peter B. Waite's *The Man from Halifax: Sir John Thompson, Prime Minister*, in referring to Charles Tupper as being "aggressively sexual."

other than his wife. We never hear Mercy mention anything like that about Tupper, and Margaret Gray's account here seems like a tame recounting of a simple and friendly request, but who knows? Perhaps there is more to this story than meets the eye.

Margaret Gray kept extensive diaries, thirty of which have been preserved. The one from 1864 has not been found. Margaret married Artemus Lord, a businessman and civil servant, about 1870. She died in 1941, at ninety-six.

William McDougall's daughter Jessie is the one with whom Mercy goes shopping. McDougall's biography lists his children thus: "William McDougall had six children: George, Harold, Gladwyn, Dr. Westroppe, Mrs. George Brown, and Mrs. Alfred Seymour." Mrs. Seymour turns out to be the Jessie in question, and though listed last, she was his first-born daughter. She was only sixteen during the Quebec conference, and married Alfred Seymour in 1870, at age twenty-two. William McDougall became lieutenant-governor designate of the North-Western Territory in 1869, and went out to Pembina, Manitoba, early in the fall of that year. He took four of his children, as he'd just been widowed. It's not known whether Jessie was one of them. McDougall's job was to help transfer the land of the Hudson's Bay Company to become part of the new North-West Territories; his handling of the affair started the Red River Rebellion.

McDougall's right-hand man in setting up the Boundary Commission in the Red River was Major Donald Cameron. Charles Tupper's daughter Emma had married Donald Cameron in July of 1869. She went with Cameron to Pembina, and was pregnant at the end of 1869. Cameron had a run-in with Louis Riel, and Riel had taken their belongings. Tupper, in his autobiography, *Recollections of Sixty Years in Canada*, which reads like a *Boys' Own* adventure novel, writes of how he travelled from Nova Scotia to Pembina, by horse and foot, across the prairie plains day and night, in the cold and dark winter, to "rescue" her. He arrived on Emma's doorstep at midnight on Christmas Eve. Tupper says she asked him what he was doing there.

Emma and Cameron set up an estate, Emmadale, in Manitoba. They had seven children. The first one, Sophie Tupper Cameron, was born in Halifax at the end of April 1870, and so Emma must have returned home to have the baby, as her father and mother wanted.

Emma Tupper, October 29, 1864, in a photograph by William Notman. The portrait is a negative that had not been digitized before, and was discovered by the McCord Museum during this research into Emma Tupper.

Thomas Haviland's widowed sister, Mrs. Alexander, was the only other single woman from PEI, aside from Mercy Coles and Margaret Gray, who went to the Quebec conference. She also vied for Leonard Tilley's attention. Her name was Mary Alice Brecken Haviland. She'd married Thomas Alexander in 1856 in England, and he'd died in 1860, so they were married just four years, and she'd been widowed another four before the Quebec Confederation conference. She did not marry again, and passed away in London, England, in 1881, at fifty-seven. Her father died in 1867, and he left a substantial sum of money to each of his children.

Two of William Henry Steeves's daughters went to Quebec. He had four daughters, the first three of whom would be about the right age to have accompanied him. Henrietta was born about 1838; Martha Jane in 1840; Lucinda in 1842; and Caroline (Carrie) was born in 1850. (Steeves's two sons were born in 1846 and 1848.) According to family history, it was Carrie who went to Quebec, even though she was only fourteen. A cushion made from one of her dresses is displayed at the Steeves House Museum in New Brunswick.* As she was just fourteen, it would seem likely that the sisters who didn't go were spoken for. That may have been the case at the time, but the two older ones did not marry until 1870 and 1883. The third daughter, Lucinda, also married in 1883. In *Samphire Greens: The story of the Steeves*, Esther Clark Wright, a famous Atlantic Canadian historian in the mid-1900s, says Lucinda married an elderly man in Torquay, England. When William Steeves died in 1873, his wife took all six of the children, the four girls and two boys — who could hardly be considered children anymore — to England, where Steeves's brother, Gilbert, lived. Wright says the three who married were all widowed soon after marriage, and Lucinda was the only one to have a child. Caroline never married, and at fourteen, she was the youngest of all of the women who went to the Quebec Confederation conference. Which one of Caroline's other three sisters went is unknown, though perhaps it was Lucinda, as the

* The cushion was on display at the Canadian Museum of History in Gatineau until January 2016 for its "1867: Rebellion and Confederation" exhibit. The Notman photograph of Mercy Coles was also displayed there, as was her diary; these artifacts are now part of the travelling "1867: Rebellion and Confederation" exhibit.

Emma Tupper's "carte de visite" was taken from her half-length portrait. Margaret Gray said she thought Emma Tupper was the most beautiful young woman who attended the big ball on Friday, October 14.

next-youngest daughter. She would have been twenty-two years old then. Their "monopolizing" of the parlour and of Mr. Carver, the "beau of Miss Fisher's," didn't help them any, it appears.

Charles Fisher married in 1836, and had four daughters and four sons. Two daughters had "cartes de visite" done in 1865, and these two were still unmarried in 1864. Frances Amelia was twenty in 1864, and Jane Paulette Marie was twenty-four. Jane didn't marry till 1884, when she was forty-four years old, and it's likely that it was she who went to Quebec — without, ultimately, any luck with Mr. Carver either, it would seem. In 1884, she married John James Fraser, who'd been premier of New Brunswick from 1878 to 1882, and was lieutenant-governor from 1893 to 1896.

Joanna Archibald was the twenty-year-old daughter of Adams Archibald of Nova Scotia. Mercy never mentions her in the diary, aside from when she writes of the women arriving from the Maritimes on October 10. Joanna married Francis Duke Laurie in 1881, at the age of thirty-seven.

Of the daughter of Colonel John Hamilton Gray of New Brunswick, Charlotte Elizabeth, even less is known. She was likely born no earlier than 1846, as her father and mother, Elizabeth Ormond, married in 1845, and she thus may have been seventeen or eighteen in Quebec. She married Captain Henry Jardine Hallowes in 1868. He'd moved to New Brunswick in 1866 to help fight the Fenian invasions there, and was adjutant general. Charlotte must have met him then, and they married within two years.

Of the ten single women who went to the Quebec conference, two, Mercy Coles and Caroline Steeves, never married, and Mrs. Alexander didn't remarry. Three married fairly late: Joanna Archibald at thirty-seven, Lucinda Steeves at forty-one, and Jane Fisher at forty-four. If it was one of Lucinda's other sisters who went to Quebec, both of them married late, too — Henrietta at thirty-two years of age, and Martha at forty-three. One wonders whether there was a dearth of young men, or an excess of young women, in these women's circles.

Of the single men Mercy wrote of, Charles Drinkwater married within four years, and Hewitt Bernard never married. The two widowers,

John A. Macdonald and Leonard Tilley, both remarried in 1867, three years after the conference in Quebec.

History continues, of course. It is these women's children who took part in the First World War. It is our own grandfathers who may have fought in World War One; people who we may remember. We are not as far from the past as we may feel; the more we look back, the closer the past becomes.

# Conclusion

I was born in Quebec in 1960, and grew up just outside of Montreal. I turned seven during Expo 67. Seven is a magic and seminal age in a child's life, when the irrational turns to rational, when suddenly you are grown, at school, learning of things outside yourself. Expo, and its impact on the world, on my family — the essential fun of it, the very being of it — was magic: the irrational and the rational; La Ronde and the world's pavilions, in a heady mixture that was the centre of our world that year; my sisters and I receiving everything Expo that Christmas.

In the 1960s, Canadians took another step toward separating from Britain, with a new flag for Canada, and, in 1965, a new — well, renamed — airline, Air Canada. The ability to fly on larger commercial jets revolutionized travel in the 1960s, similar to the way affordable train travel in the 1860s changed the face of North America. Expo 67, the largest international exposition on North American soil, was held in Canada, where the world came calling.

And then came the FLQ crisis, and our sudden upheaval from Quebec. We moved from our house, away from all that was home, to western Ontario —

nothing like the world that was. The loss of home, the loss of Canada. My mother, born in Quebec, felt bereft at the loss, and thus I did, too.

Just after that, in 1968, Pierre Trudeau took the stage, and romanced the world. Trudeaumania flourished: the red rose, the new symbol of Canada, to me as magic as Expo 67. He came to our Girl Guide event for Citizenship Day in Sarnia. I remember being close enough to touch him. Here I was, living a mixed-up mythology of Canada. The flamboyancy of Pierre Trudeau, with his "fuddle duddle," and "Just watch me," and his late love affair with and marriage to a younger woman, mimicking John A. Macdonald's flair and earthiness, and his marriage, too, to someone considerably younger than himself at the age of fifty-plus.

Not that summer of 1967, of course (when Expo was everything), but almost every other summer, we went to Prince Edward Island to visit my grandmother and aunts and uncles, and to swim those beguiling north shore beaches the 1864 newspapers wrote of. We made excursions to the country. We travelled by ferry, and saw those same green fields and red sand cliffs that rolled down to the sea. The green leather seats of the ferries, like the seats in Province House. *Anne of Green Gables,* a song in Charlottetown, and a babbling brook in Cavendish. It was summer — the weather was always beautiful, and when it wasn't, it smelled of islands and summer, of Canada.

I couldn't help but be taken with the Confederation story once I heard it. Like Mercy Coles, I couldn't help myself or stop myself.

---

In reading the Mercy Coles diary, I admit what caught my eye were things like "John A. brought me my dessert in the drawing room. The conundrum." And, "I wonder if they are thinking of me this morning? Mr. Tilley will have enough to do taking care of Mrs. Alexander." Who wouldn't be intrigued? Was this a budding romance? The relationships in our own lives make up who we are. Who we love and loved, who loves us and when; these are some of the essential ingredients of our lives. We live longer and happier lives when we have good connections with people. The research is clear: our relationships with others, and how we live, affect the tenor, the health, even the very span of our lives.

How can we possibly understand our history if we don't look at the relationships of individuals, and their connections with people? That John A. Macdonald or Leonard Tilley may have been interested in Mercy Coles, that she may have been interested in them, or that she thought they were interested in her, makes those ever-important social events in Charlottetown and Quebec all the more crucial to know from other perspectives, not only those of the men known to history.

# Acknowledgements

A special thanks to Christopher Moore, from whom I first heard of the Mercy Coles diary, and much thanks also to the CBC radio program *Ideas* on which he was speaking. Chris has also been generous in answering many questions on the politics and people of Confederation.

I am especially indebted to Professor Ed MacDonald, chair of the History Department at the University of Prince Edward Island. He helpfully answered many and sundry questions, even a last-minute one on Christmas Eve. He was informative on Islanders' stance on the American Civil War, and was very helpful in identifying and providing background and resources on some of the PEI men Mercy wrote of.

I thank the Gabriel Dumont Institute Library staff at the University of Regina for their generous support and research on Louis Riel, and in particular for finding information on the "Daughters of Confederation," the young unmarried women who went along with their fathers or brothers to the Quebec Confederation conference in October 1864.

Nora Hague, William Notman scholar at the McCord Museum in Montreal, was an indispensable source of information on Notman, and without her help I doubt the photograph of Mercy Coles would have been found. I also thank Heather McNabb at the McCord Museum, who discovered the full portrait negatives of Hewitt Bernard and Emma Tupper and provided very useful information on Notman and portrait photography at the time.

A very special thanks goes to the Canadian Museum of History in Gatineau, Quebec, for providing their excellent photocopies of the first pages of the Mercy Coles diary reproduced here, as well as curator Jean-François Lozier and collections information specialist Vincent Lafond.

My thanks to Dr. Christopher Rutty who provided information on the fight against diphtheria in Canada; to Thomas Flanagan for information he provided me on Louis Riel, and for informing me that none of Riel's papers from 1864 survive; to Sam McBride who provided information and insight into his ancestors Colonel John Hamilton Gray and Margaret Gray Lord of Prince Edward Island. See Christopher Rutty's HealthHeritageResearch website, and Sam McBride's blog, TheBravestCanadian.

Special thanks go also to my sister Margaret Brady for her helpful suggestions on a final draft of this manuscript; to the rest of my family for their ongoing encouragement; and to Gord Hunter who hosted me in Montreal while I researched at the McCord Museum. And thanks always to my husband, David Sealy, for his support and help in whatever is needed — from commas to champagne.

Finally, much thanks goes to the people of Dundurn Press, especially to my insightful editor, Dominic Farrell, and all the production and marketing staff, for their enthusiasm for this book.

# Appendix

*"Reminiscences of Confederation Days: Extracts from a Diary Kept by Miss Mercy A. Coles When She Accompanied Her Father, the Late Hon. George Coles, to the Confederation Conferences in Quebec, Montreal and Ottawa in 1864."*

In connection with the celebration of the Jubilee of Confederation, the following extracts from the diary of Miss Mercy A. Coles of this city, who as a young girl accompanied her father and mother, the late Hon. George Coles and Mrs. Coles to the preliminary conferences, will be of peculiar interest.

# Extracts from Diary

The delegates from Quebec, Halifax and St John arrived in Charlottetown on August 30,* 1864 and held their first meeting in the Council Chamber. Dr. Tupper (afterwards Sir Charles) came to see us and said that a party of them had had an enjoyable ride and a shoot that was more amusing than profitable. This excursion was, if not immortalized, at least commemorated by the Island Bard, the late John LePage.

On August 31 there was a highly successful banquet when a good many speeches were made. I went into supper with Mr. McDougall (afterwards Sir William) who was a very nice man. Mr. J.A. McDonald (afterwards Sir John) made a speech. On September 1st, all of the delegates had their photographs taken on the steps of the Government House. Major Bernard and Mr. Drinkwater, Sir John's secretaries, and Mr. Lea, Clerk at the Council, were asked to dinner at Government House. The conference meetings were held every day beginning at mid-day.

[This description of the delegates and Mercy's trip to Nova Scotia and New Brunswick starts on Friday, September 9]

With my father and the other delegates we crossed to Pictou and after going around and seeing the town we went to a small museum where the only thing I saw that was really worth looking at was a piece of amethyst found in Nova Scotia. It was nearly as large as a child's head. There were a few other old-fashioned curiosities there. After dinner we went to Stellarton and Mr. Hudson, the manager of the mine, invited us to tea. Some of the gentlemen went down into the mine; I was asked to go but it looked too dirty and black. We went in coaches to Truro and did not arrive until 10 o'clock. The drive was long and dreary. Mrs.

* The Canadians arrived on Thursday, September 1. Mercy has a number of dates and days wrong in this extract.

Archibald (afterwards lady), wife of Sir Thomas Archibald* Governor of Nova Scotia, invited the whole party to supper but it was too late to go. We stayed at Truro all night and in the morning set out for Halifax. We stopped at the Waverly gold mines, a weird looking place, which someone remarked was the place where Noah flung out the ballast. They gave me a piece of gold quartz. I met an interesting lady, a Mrs. Greenhow, who is travelling incognito with her secretary whom she called her son. She had been in Paris and London and had interviews with Napoleon and Lord Shaftesbury soliciting aid for the sufferers in the south. I thought by what she said that she had received a good deal of money. She showed me her dresses, one of which was magnificent, made in Paris. (Note: Miss Coles has a letter and photograph afterwards received from Mrs. Greenhow, and also a later letter telling of her death. She was drowned while trying to land with a little boat. The boat swamped when near shore and while others managed to land Mrs. Greenhow, owing to the weight of a lot of gold that she had tied around her waist, was drowned. Her body was laid to rest in the church yard at Richmond.)

At night we dined at Government House. Sir Richard and Lady MacDonnell (Mr. Malachi Daly was his secretary) were there. They were very kind. Government House was an old-fashioned place, not nearly so nice as Charlottetown.

I spent a day on board the flagship *Duncan* on September [illegible]. In the morning it rained and I had a note from the admiral who had asked me to go, saying it was too wet for ship visiting. However it cleared at lunchtime and he sent his lieutenant.

On the night of September 12 there was a banquet at the Halifax Hotel. I dined at Mrs. McCully's, wife of one of the delegates. When I got home, they were still giving speeches at the banquet. We went to church on the morning of the 14th (Sunday).** Dr. Tupper called and took us to the service, which was held in a hall, as St. Paul's was being

* Sir Thomas Adams Archibald.

** September 14 would have been Wednesday. The events line up with Peter Waite's descriptions in his *Life and Times of Confederation, 1864–1867*, but Mercy has her days of the week wrong.

repaired. The doctor showed me a photograph of his daughter who had died of diphtheria. She was a lovely child and he felt for her death very much. On Monday we took a boat to St. John and enjoyed a very pleasant trip. The captain took the steamer quite close to Bird Rock that I might see the millions of birds on it. The rock seemed to be covered with snow, the birds being perfectly white. On Tuesday [Friday] the 16th the whole party except myself went over to Fredericton. Mr. and Mrs. Thomas Morris, then a bride and groom, were with me. I drove to the Suspension Bridge and round the Asylum with Miss Reid. The Reids had a beautiful place outside St. John, "Reid's Castle."* The delegates came back in the evening.

The date of the conference at Quebec having been fixed, the Governor decided to send a steamer down to bring the delegates up from the Maritime Provinces. I went via St. John and Portland as my father thought the trip would be too rough for mother and me. On Wednesday, October 5, we left Charlottetown at 8 AM and arrived at Shediac at 2:30 PM. It was terribly rough and I became ill. We found a special train waiting for us at Shediac and we got into St. John at 6:30 in the evening. Mr. Tilley (afterwards Sir Leonard) and Mr. Steeves were at the hotel to receive us. On Thursday we went on board the steamer *New Brunswick*. Mrs. Alexander and I had a state room. We arrived at Preble House, Portland, the following morning after 24 hours on the steamer. At 1 o'clock we went on the Grand Trunk railway arriving at Island Pond at 9:30. A quaint old building, the hotel was three-storied.

Mr. Tilley was very kind to our party. He was the only gentlemen among five ladies and he had quite a lot to do to keep them all in good humor. On Sunday afternoon we arrived in Quebec at about half-past five. There was no one to meet us and we drove to the Russell House. The whole hotel was given out to the party and the arrangements for their comfort were very complete. We had a suite of rooms opposite the parlour which

* The family name was Reed, not Reid.

was occupied by Mr. George Brown and his secretary, Mr. Hubertos. The St. John delegates had a parlour which they shared with the Prince Edward Island delegates. After dressing for dinner we went downstairs and found Mr. Brown in the drawing room. Colonel Bernard had been in a few minutes before. After a short while George E. Cartier, Mr. J.A. McDonald, and Mr. D'Arcy McGee arrived. Before dinner was announced we were introduced in the Newfoundland delegates, the Honourable Ambrose Shea and Mr. Carter* who took us to dinner. We had a splendid dinner and I enjoyed it. We had been travelling in cars from 6:30 AM until 5:30 PM. From Richmond to Somerset we went at the rate of only 9 miles an hour. A special train met us there and we went on to point Levis, crossed [by] ferry and landed at the wharf in Quebec.

I can hardly describe my first impression of Quebec. It was pouring rain when we landed and three of us took a little cab. The horses stumbled a good deal owing to the steepness of the hills. However, we reached the hotel all right. It was a very nice hotel with every comfort one could wish for. We had a drive around Spencer Wood, a very pretty place. We did not go into the cemetery. It was something strange to see quite a good deal of snow on the ground, for it was early in the season.

On Sunday morning we went to the Cathedral, where Bishop Williams preached. The music was very good. The organist was quite talented. Father and mother and Mr. Tilley and I sat together. Major Bernard told me later at the hotel that we were to have an excellent time throughout the week and that there was to be a Reception on Tuesday and a public ball on Friday. Mrs. Penny invited mother and me to visit her. Mr. Galt, Mr. Cartier, Mr. Couchon, Mr. Cameron and a lot of other gentlemen were there, and Mr. Galt gave me a warm welcome to Canada. On Monday night the steamer arrived with the other delegates who showed signs of fatigue. Among the party were the two Misses Gray (daughter of Colonel Gray of P.E.I. and daughter of Colonel Gray of St. John), Mrs. and Miss Tupper, Mrs. and Miss Archibald. Mr. McDougall (afterwards Sir William) brought his daughter to see me and we went out shopping together. After lunch Mr. Drinkwater (Sir John's secretary), mother and I went for a drive. We went

* Frederick Carter was the other Newfoundland delegate.

to the Cathedral then to the Seminary Chapel to see the fine paintings. Afterwards we drove to the Provincial Building to see what the library was like; it did not strike us as being very wonderful. On our return Mrs. Campbell, wife of Hon. Mr. Campbell, called on mother and me. When the gentlemen came from the Conference they brought cards of invitation to Mrs. and Miss Tupper and Miss Gray to dine at Government House. Mother and I have a card for Wednesday. The organist of the Cathedral, a Mr. Pierce, called on us; he was a very nice man. Mr. McDougall and his daughter, Jessie, dined with us. Father and all the gentlemen who were not dining at Government House were dining at the Stadacona Club. On the night of Wednesday, October 12, we went down to the drawing room where quite a number of ladies were assembled. Several gentlemen wanted to take me into the room. The Governor General Lord Monck stood in the middle of the room with his private secretary at his right. The aide-de-camp announced us each in turn and the governor shook hands with us in a friendly manner. About 800 persons were presented. I was very tired before it was all over. There were refreshments in a room adjoining. On the following day we went to see the falls at Lorette and the Indian Chief. It was raining and so we did not go down into the gorge. Colonel Gray led the party. We went into the Chief's house; it was not what I had expected to see. The only thing Indian about it was a tomahawk. I bought a wooden spoon to take home as a curio. The Old Chief was the last of the Huron Tribe. He had two silver medals presented by King George IV and one by the Prince of Wales. In the evening we dined at the Governor General's. Mr. Thomas D'Arcy McGee took me to dinner and sat between Lady McDonald* and me. On Thursday night Mr. Sala, the great English journalist, dined with us. I was rather disappointed in the man, a rough red-faced Englishman, black hair and black eyes. Mr. George Brown sat near me and introduced me to him.

On Thursday afternoon mother and I went for a walk on Durham Terrace. While there a large piece of rock fell. At first we thought the house nearby was on fire, owing to the great amount of dust that arose. When

---

* This should be Lady MacDonnell, wife of Sir Richard MacDonnell, lieutenant-governor of Nova Scotia.

the gentlemen came home from the conference they said that the rock had pierced the roof of the house and killed a child in a cradle. (Note: the sore throat which troubled her regrettably developed into diphtheria and Miss Coles could not attend the ball. She however obtained a description of it from her mother and others from which the following is taken.) The young ladies came up to see me next morning and said I had not missed much. The ball was rather a failure so far as the delegates were concerned. The Quebec people never introduced either the ladies or the gentlemen to any partners, nor did they see whether or not they were provided for as regards supper. The Grays were indignant at the manner in which their daughters were treated. Miss Gray and Miss Tupper came to see me; they went to Mount Morency* on Saturday. Mr. Livesay accompanied them.

The bachelors of Quebec had a ball in the Provincial Building. We were invited to a party on the following evening. On Wednesday mother, father, and I went to visit the Ursuline Convent. There was a brilliant ball at Madame Tessier's. Father came home and said he had never had such a time before. There was only one Island lady there. Mr. Lea, Clerk of the Council, paid me a visit on Friday afternoon; he was the first gentleman who came to see me in my sickness. The conference met at 12 o'clock and adjourned at 6 o'clock. I was very much better and could go into the parlor. I learned that Mr. John A. had been making enquiries about me. Mr. Livesay also sent me a very kind message. Mr. J.A. Macdonald dined with us at night. After dinner he entertained me with small talk and gave me a conundrum: "Why were he and Mrs. Alexander like two Roman generals?" The answer was "She's Alexander and I sees her (Caesar)." On the following morning I went out for a drive and remained out an hour. We did not go in at any place. Mr. Livesay gave me his photograph. He looks so venerable with his white hair. (This photograph is still in the position of Miss Coles.) I had quite a collection of photographs, for every gentleman sent me his. (Among the most valuable of Miss Coles' treasures is an album containing the photographs of the ladies and gentlemen she met at the conference including the delegates and many of the citizens of Quebec.) I went down to luncheon and had some Malpeque oysters from the Island; it was the first

* This is Montmorency Falls.

thing I enjoyed during my illness. We were told that we were positively to start from Montreal on the next Thursday.

On Wednesday I went for a drive to see where it was that the rock had fallen and killed a child. At dinner in the evening Sir John sat next to me. We left for Montreal as expected on Thursday, where I received a letter from home. We reached the St. Lawrence Hotel at night, half past ten. On the advice of Dr. Tupper the ladies, instead of going by the midnight train, took steamer. On arriving at the hotel I was surprised to find that I was the invalid for whom preparations have been made. Evidently Mr. Macdonald, who had always proved a very kind friend to me, had telegraphed ahead. I found the room, which had been assigned to me, equipped with a large fireplace. They must have been somewhat astonished to see the invalid acting in such a spritely way as I did. The hotel was immense. On Friday night, October 29, I attended a splendid ball and danced with Mr. Crowther in the first quadrille. General Williams called on us all in the afternoon. I had seen him before in Charlottetown; he was "the Hero of Kars." I did not stay very late at the dance, although I was engaged for several dances; but mother and father remained. Mother told me when she came home the ball was a great success. They showed me the menu card. (A souvenir of this ball in the shape of a white satin program is in the position of Miss Coles.) Mr. Andrew McDonald,* Colonel Gray, and Mrs. Pope and mother and I went to Notman's studio. It was an elaborate photographic studio. We were on board the *Prince of Wales* on Monday morning, October 31, on the Ottawa River. We left Montreal at 7 o'clock that morning when we saw the rapids mentioned in the Canadian boat song. We made the acquaintance of a Mr. Robertson who offered us his place at the Cathedral, in which we saw the Bible presented by the Prince of Wales. We went up to the McGill College in the vicinity of which there were magnificent residences, and then back to the hotel in the street car. At the hotel we took an omnibus to go for a drive over the Victoria Bridge. One of the ladies came down to the door and said she would not go in the omnibus, and while arguing in favour of a carriage, her husband stepped into the omnibus, leaving her standing at the door. We passed through Griffin town, a very muddy place, and chaffed Mr. McGee on the state of his constituency. At the

* Andrew Macdonald.

bridge we got out and looked at the last rivet in the construction work; it was a silver rivet which the Prince of Wales had driven when he was in Canada. They opened the windows and we looked down on a raft of timber which was just then passing under the bridge. It was a lovely day and we enjoyed the outing immensely. On November 1st we were in Ottawa. In the picture gallery of the parliament building we had luncheon. It was a pleasant affair, and some of the men made speeches, my father being among them. He was speaking of the allurements they were going to hold out to the Maritime Provinces to enter Confederation. Father horrified mother and me by saying that among the fine things we had down here, we had the finest looking ladies, pointing to mother as a specimen. The other gentleman said equally ridiculous things. After luncheon we saw a model of the library; it consisted of plaster. We went to the top of the building which commanded a view of the Chaudière Falls. In the evening we attended an elaborate ball which we all enjoyed very much, but I left with half a dozen engagements to be fulfilled. Mr. Bridges [Brydges] bet me that mother was lying on the sofa and I bet him that she was not, and I won. We arrived at Toronto at 10 o'clock. A crowd of about five thousand was in front of the hotel, and speeches were made from the gallery. Next morning we went to see the public institutions. All the older boys of the public school turned out when the headmaster read an address and Colonel Gray of P.E. Island replied. In honour of the occasion the boys were given a holiday. We saw the Lawyers' Hall, a magnificent building. The students wore caps and gowns. We next paid a visit to the museum where we saw some beautiful butterflies. The Normal School was a sort of "variety" institution, combining all sorts of things. We had to hurry back to the hotel. Mother and I went shopping. Colonel Bernard was awaiting in the parlour when we came home and he took us to dinner. At night we had a splendid dance; the ladies were very attractive in their pretty dresses. We did not get home until 3 o'clock. On the following day most of the party went to Toronto while we went to Ohio. I did not see Mr. J.A. Macdonald, but Mr. Bernard said he had asked him to say goodbye. At Buffalo we saw the falls; a Mr. Swinyard accompanied us. We bought curiosities at exorbitant prices and then we drove to Street's Gardens, with their beautiful grounds. After seeing all there was to be seen, we drove to the station and said good-bye. The Tuppers went to New York and the others went on to Toronto.

# Note on Sources

The full transcription of Mercy Coles's original diary, a photocopy of which is held by Library and Archives Canada, is included here. As noted, this is the first time this diary has been published in full. As a reference and comparison, I've also included, in the appendix, a transcription of the newspaper article titled "Reminiscences of Confederation Days: Extracts from a Diary Kept by Miss Mercy A. Coles When She Accompanied Her Father, the Late Hon. George Coles, to the Confederation Conferences at Quebec, Montreal and Ottawa in 1864." Interestingly, this extract has some notable omissions, errors, and additions to the original diary document. I've noted many of those throughout the book.

This book is, I believe, the only place in which Mercy and her family's two weeks of visiting and travel back home from the Quebec conference, through the United States during the Civil War, is documented.

For overall understanding of the political landscape, and background to Confederation, I read many books on Maritime history: Ian Ross Robertson's *The Tenant League of Prince Edward Island, 1864–67*; W.M. Whitelaw's older work from the 1930s; and, of course, Francis Bolger's *Prince*

*Edward Island and Confederation: 1863–1873*. For additional information on Confederation I read Donald Creighton's *The Road to Confederation: The Emergence of Canada, 1863–1867*; biographies of John A. Macdonald by Donald Swainson, Donald Creighton, and Richard Gwyn; and Joseph Pope's work on the correspondence of Macdonald. In particular, I am indebted to Christopher Moore's *1867: How the Fathers Made a Deal*, and to Peter B. Waite's *The Life and Times of Confederation, 1864–1867*, first published by University of Toronto Press in 1962, a crucial resource for anyone exploring Canada's Confederation. Waite used the newspaper reports of the day to comment informatively, and eloquently, on everything to do with Confederation. Both books have been indispensable resources.

Mary McDonald-Rissanen's work on women diarists found in *In the Interval of the Wave: Prince Edward Island Women's Nineteenth- and Early Twentieth-Century Life Writing*, and Joanne Findon's *Seeking Our Eden: The Dreams and Migrations of Sarah Jameson Craig*, along with Kathryn Carter's *The Small Details of Life: 20 Diaries by Women in Canada, 1830–1996*, which I read selectively, helped shape my understanding of women's writing in the period in which Mercy Coles was writing.

For "Charlottetown: The Circus, Champagne, and Union," I made use of a number of primary sources, such as the PEI newspapers, and George Brown's letters written to his wife, Anne, in September of 1864, found in the George Brown fonds at Library and Archives Canada. Francis Bolger's *Prince Edward Island and Confederation: 1863–1873* was very helpful for my understanding of PEI's limited pro-Confederation stance.

Jamie Bradburn, in the blog *The Torontoist*, on April 11, 2012, offers one of the livelier, and also more succinct, explanations of the Great Coalition. Bradburn quotes W.L. Morton's book *The Critical Years*. See http://torontoist.com/2011/04/goin_down_the_coalition_road/.

I made extensive use of C.M. Wallace's biography of Leonard Tilley, found in the *Dictionary of Canadian Biography*, throughout "The Journey Begins: The Lure of Travel, the New — and Leonard Tilley."

The *DCB* was invaluable for its biographies of Hewitt Bernard, George Brown, George Coles, Charles Fisher, Alexander Galt, John A. Macdonald, Susan Agnes Bernard Macdonald, William McDougall, Lord Monck, William Pope, Joseph Pope, William Steeves, Leonard Tilley, and Charles Tupper, among others.

For “From the Sublime to the Ridiculous: The “Failed,” the Grand Success, or the Drunken Fiasco of the Government Ball: Thursday, October 13 to Monday, October 17,” I used Frances Elizabeth Owen (Feo) Monck’s unedited journal, which is a wealth of information about Canada’s social side, and a fascinating read. It is found in W.L. Morton, *Monck Letters and Journals 1863–1868: Canada from Government House at Confederation*, published by McClelland and Stewart in 1970.

Throughout the book, and, in particular, in both “Diphtheria” and “The Temptation of John A. Macdonald: Thursday, October 20 to Wednesday, October 26,” Hewitt Bernard’s minutes of the conference, found in G.P. Browne’s *Documents on the Confederation of British North America,* were useful. From the minutes, I have noted who Bernard reported as absent from the talks, and for what reason. Bernard’s minutes also provide information on the conference discussions, and on voting.

In “What She Said — A Woman’s Point of View,” I used Feo Monck’s unedited journal and Peter B. Waite’s article “Edward Whelan Reports from the Quebec Conference,” found in the *Canadian Historical Review* XLII, 1961.

“Montreal Sightseeing and the ‘Eighth Wonder of the World’: Thursday, October 27 to Monday, October 31” owes much to the McCord Museum’s online display of photographs and information on the Victoria Bridge. Elaine Kalman Naves’s two-episode documentary for CBC’s *Ideas* (May 2012) on William Notman was also integral to the portrayal of Notman here.

The firsthand accounts of the American Civil War in “Family and Travel: Saturday, November 5 to Thursday, November 10” are from two online sites with extensive information and primary source material. The Charles Caley Civil War letter is housed at the University of Notre Dame, in Indiana. The university has a significant collection of Civil War correspondence, which can be found online. The excerpts from Henry Hitchcock’s diary, and General Sherman’s writings, are found on the GeorgiaInfo website.

For the Prince Edward Islanders’ stance on the Civil War, Professor Ed MacDonald was informative, and helpfully suggested the piece from the *Islander* magazine, “Soldiers of Liberty: Islanders and the Civil War,” by Greg Marquis.

In "Going Home: Thursday, November 10 to Thursday, November 17," the quotations from George Coles, and information on his deteriorating state of health, are found in T.H. Holman's article in *The Island Magazine* 29, Spring/Summer 1991: 20–22.

For the final chapter on the "Daughters of Confederation," I used many genealogical sources. I searched wherever I could, and made my best estimates by examining all the material that I found. It was a challenging process, as information varied from source to source. I used the Ancestry.ca website, family genealogical sites, and histories of the fathers and mothers of the women I was researching, as well as family histories and local histories. I think I found everything that could be found, although I am sure there must still be many mementos, and perhaps "cartes" — the photographs taken by the famous photographers of the day — out there yet, treasured by the relatives of these "Daughters of Confederation."

# Notes

***Chapter One: Miss Confederation***

1. Mercy Anne Coles, *Reminiscences of Canada in 1864* (diary), R2663-0-6-E, Library and Archives Canada (hereafter cited as Coles diary).
2. "Reminiscences of Confederation Days: Extracts from a Diary Kept by Miss Mercy A. Coles When She Accompanied Her Father, the Late Hon. George Coles, to the Confederation Conferences at Quebec, Montreal and Ottawa in 1864," *Charlottetown Guardian*, June 30, 1917 (hereafter cited as "Extracts from a Diary").
3. Evelyn MacLeod, *One Woman's Charlottetown: Diaries of Margaret Gray Lord, 1863, 1876, 1890* (Ottawa: Canadian Museum of Civilization, 1988), 53.
4. Quoted in Christopher Moore, *Three Weeks in Quebec City: The Meeting That Made Canada*, History of Canada Series (Toronto: Allen Lane, 2015), 1.
5. Douglas Baldwin and Thomas Spira, eds., *Gaslights, Epidemics and Vagabond Cows: Charlottetown in the Victorian Era* (Charlottetown: Ragweed Press, 1988), 30.
6. MacLeod, *One Woman's Charlottetown*, 50.

7. Ibid., 15.
8. George Brown to Anne Brown, 5 September 1864, George Brown Fonds, R2634 0-9-E, Library and Archives Canada.
9. Coles diary.
10. Peter B. Waite, "Edward Whelan Reports from the Quebec Conference," *Canadian Historical Review* XLII (1961): 41.

***Chapter Two: Charlottetown***

1. George Brown to Anne Brown, 2 September 1864.
2. Ibid., 5 September 1864.

***Chapter Three: The Journey Begins***

1. W.M. Whitelaw, "Reconstructing the Quebec Conference," *Canadian Historical Review* XIX (1938): 131.
2. C.M. Wallace, "Tilley, Sir Samuel Leonard," *Dictionary of Canadian Biography*, vol. 12, University of Toronto/Université Laval, 2003, www.biographi.ca/en/bio/tilley_samuel_leonard_12E.html.

***Chapter Four: From the Sublime to the Ridiculous***

1. Edward Whelan, *The Union of the British Provinces* (1865; repr., Toronto: Garden City Press, 1927), 67–68.

***Chapter Six: The Temptation of John A. Macdonald***

1. Waite, "Edward Whelan Reports from the Quebec Conference," 41.
2. From the Charlottetown *Islander*, March 17, 1865, which was reporting on the PEI Assembly debates of March 2, 1865. As reported in Peter B. Waite, *The Life and Times of Confederation 1864–1867* (Toronto: University of Toronto Press, 1962; repr., 1977), page 83, footnote 45.
3. Whelan, *Union*, 138.
4. Joseph Pope, "24 March 1865," *Correspondence of Sir John Macdonald* (Toronto: Doubleday, Page, 1921).

***Chapter Eight: Montreal Sightseeing and the "Eighth Wonder of the World"***

1. William Notman, *Photography: Things You Ought to Know* (n.p., n.d., ca. 1866–67).

### *Chapter Nine: Ottawa the Unseemly*

1. Waite, *Life and Times*, 100.
2. Whelan, *Union*, 147.

### *Chapter Ten: Sightseeing in Toronto, 1864 Style*

1. Whelan, *Union,* 166.

### *Chapter Eleven: Niagara Falls*

1. W.L. Morton, *Monck Letters and Journals, 1863–1868: Canada from Government House at Confederation* (Toronto: McClelland and Stewart, 1970), 147.

### *Chapter Twelve: Family and Travel*

1. MacLeod, *One Woman's Charlottetown*, 2.

# Bibliography


***Primary Sources***

"And Still They Come." *Vindicator* (Charlottetown), September 7, 1864.

"Ball and Banquet." *Ross's Weekly* (Charlottetown), September 15, 1864.

Brown, George. Letters of George Brown to Anne Brown. George Brown Fonds. R26340-9-E. Library and Archives Canada.

Browne, G.P., ed. *Documents on the Confederation of British North America.* Toronto: McClelland and Stewart, 1969.

Caley, Charles. Autograph letter, 18 December 1864. MSN CW 5024-27. Rare Books and Special Collections, University of Notre Dame.

Coles, Mercy Ann. *Reminiscences of Canada in 1864* (diary). R2663-0-6-E. Library and Archives Canada.

"Excursion of the Delegates to Niagara Falls." *Globe* (Toronto, Canada West), November 5, 1864.

GeorgiaInfo. "This Day in Georgia Civil War History: November 15, 1864." http://georgiainfo.galileo.usg.edu/thisday/cwhistory/11/15/march-to-the-sea-began-battle-of-stockbridge-burning-of-atlanta.

GeorgiaInfo. "This Day in Georgia Civil War History: November 16, 1864." http://georgiainfo.galileo.usg.edu/thisday/cwhistory/11/16/

sherman-departed-atlanta-on-march-to-the-sea.
Notman, William. Photographic Archives. McCord Museum, Montreal.
———. *Photography: Things You Ought to Know*. N.p.: n.d., ca. 1866–67.
"Reception of the Delegates." *Charlottetown Islander*, September 2, 1864.
"Reminiscences of Confederation Days: Extracts from a Diary Kept by Miss Mercy A. Coles When She Accompanied Her Father, the Late Hon. George Coles, to the Confederation Conferences at Quebec, Montreal and Ottawa in 1864." *Charlottetown Guardian*, June 30, 1917.
"She Saw Canada Born." *Winnipeg Free Press*, September 1, 1937.
"Unexpected Death of Miss Mercy A. Coles." *Charlottetown Guardian*, February 12, 1921.

### *Secondary Sources*

Baldwin, Douglas, and Thomas Spira, eds. *Gaslights, Epidemics and Vagabond Cows: Charlottetown in the Victorian Era*. Charlottetown: Ragweed Press, 1988.
Blake, Raymond, Jeffrey Keshen, Norman Knowles, and Barbara Messamore. *Narrating a Nation: Canadian History Pre-Confederation*: Whitby, ON: McGraw-Hill Ryerson Higher Education, 2011.
Bolger, Francis. *Prince Edward Island and Confederation 1863–1873*. Charlottetown: St. Dunstan's University Press, 1964.
Gwyn, Sandra. *The Private Capital: Ambition and Love in the Age of Macdonald and Laurier*. Toronto: McClelland and Stewart, 1984.
Hawkins Bell, Sue. *A Journey from Somerset, England to Ohio: For the Hawkins and Haine Family, 1700–2000*. Bloomington, IN: Xlibris, 2011.
Hodges, James. *Construction of the Great Victoria Bridge in Canada by James Hodges, Engineer, to Messrs. Peto, Brassey, and Betts, Contractors*. London: J. Weale, 1860. https://archive.org/details/cihm_45104.
Holmon, T.H. "'Deserted by God and Man': The Tragedy of George Coles." *The Island Magazine* 29 (1991): 20–22.
MacLeod, Evelyn, ed. *One Woman's Charlottetown: Diaries of Margaret Gray Lord, 1863, 1876, 1890*. Ottawa: Canadian Museum of Civilization, 1988.
Marquis, Greg. "Soldiers of Liberty: Islanders and the Civil War." *The Island Magazine* 36, Fall/Winter 1994. http://vre2.upei.ca/islandmagazine/fedora/repository/vre:islemag-batch2-478/-/Soldiers%20of%20Liberty:%20Islanders%20and%20the%20Civil%20War.

McDonald-Rissanen, Mary. *In the Interval of the Wave: Prince Edward Island Women's Nineteenth- and Early Twentieth-Century Life Writing*. Montreal: McGill-Queen's University Press, 2014.

Messamore, Barbara J. *Canada's Governors General, 1847–1878: Biography and Constitutional Evolution*. Toronto: University of Toronto Press, 2006.

Moore, Christopher. *1867: How the Fathers Made a Deal*. Toronto: McClelland and Stewart, 1997.

———. *Three Weeks in Quebec City: The Meeting That Made Canada*. History of Canada Series. Toronto: Allen Lane, 2015.

Morton, W.L. *Monck Letters and Journals, 1863–1868: Canada from Government House at Confederation*. Toronto: McClelland and Stewart, 1970.

Pope, Joseph. *Correspondence of Sir John Macdonald; Selections from the Correspondence of the Right Honourable Sir John Alexander Macdonald, G.C.B., First Prime Minister of the Dominion of Canada, Made by His Literary Executor Sir Joseph Pope*. Toronto: Doubleday, Page, 1921.

Tupper, Charles. *Recollections of Sixty Years in Canada*. Toronto: Cassels, 1914.

Waite, Peter, B. "Edward Whelan Reports from the Quebec Conference." *Canadian Historical Review* XLII (1961): 23–45.

———. *Life and Times of Confederation, 1864–1867*. Toronto: University of Toronto Press, 1962. Reprinted 1977.

Whelan, Edward, ed. *The Union of the British Provinces*. 1865. Reprinted Toronto: Garden City Press, 1927.

Whitelaw, W.M. "Reconstructing the Quebec Conference," *Canadian Historical Review*, XIX (1938): 123–37.

Wright, Esther Clark. *Samphire Greens: The Story of the Steeves*. Kingsport, NS: n.p., 1961.

# Image Credits

**All images are © McCord Museum**

27 I-13486.1 | Photograph | Miss Mercy Coles, Montreal, QC, 1864

45 I-17327.1 | Photograph | Wolfe's monument, Plains of Abraham, Quebec City, QC, 1865

46 N-0000.193.194.1 | Photograph | Place d'Armes and English Cathedral, Quebec City, QC, 1860

47 N-0000.193.16.2 | Photograph | Basilica of Notre Dame de Québec, Quebec City, QC, 1859

50 I-13477.1 | Photograph | Samuel L. Tilley, politician, Montreal, QC, 1864

55 N-0000.193.112.1 | Photograph | Lorette Falls from above the falls looking up, near Montmorency, QC, about 1860

59 N-0000.193.190.1 | Photograph | Citadel, with Wolfe and Montcalm Monument, Quebec City, QC, about 1860

61 I-12069.1 | Photograph | Lady Monck, Montreal, QC, 1864

75 I-7950 | Photograph | John A. Macdonald, politician, Montreal, QC, 1863

84 M975.62.263.3 | Wood engraving | Grand Finale of Fire-Works in Honor of the Prince of Wales and the Successful Completion of the Victoria Bridge, Montreal, Canada East

85 MP-0000.10.170 | Photograph | Bird's eye view of Seminary gardens, N-0000.193.26.1 |

88 N-0000.193.26.1 | Photograph | Christ Church Cathedral, St. Catherine Street, Montreal, QC, about 1860

94 I-16295.0 | Photograph | Parliament buildings under construction, Ottawa, ON, 1865

100 N-0000.193.213.2 | Photograph | Osgoode Hall, Toronto, ON, about 1860

142 I-4022 | Photograph | Mr. H. Bernard, Montreal, QC, 1862

145 I-23089.1 | Photograph | Charles Drinkwater, Montreal, QC, 1866

152 I-13474.1 or I-13474| Photograph | Miss Tupper, Montreal, QC, 1864

# Index